"ALL NECESSARY MEANS" - EMPLOYING CIA OPERATIVES IN A WARFIGHTING ROLE ALONGSIDE SPECIAL OPERATIONS FORCES

U.S. Army War College

TITLE: "ALL NECESSARY MEANS" – EMPLOYING CIA OPERATIVES IN A
WARFIGHTING ROLE ALONGSIDE SPECIAL OPERATIONS FORCES

In response to the terrorist attacks on the United States on 11 September 2001, the President -- as both Commander-in-Chief and as authorized by Congress in Joint Resolution 23 -- ordered our armed forces into combat in order to disrupt and defeat the global terror network. The President concomitantly signed a Presidential Finding directing the Central Intelligence Agency (CIA) to use all necessary means to destroy Osama bin Laden and Al Qaeda. As a consequence of these orders, CIA paramilitary operatives have been performing a warfighting role alongside Special Operations Forces (SOF) in the war against terrorism.

This strategy research paper explores the respective roles and missions of the CIA and SOF, their legal authority to execute their assigned missions, the policy advantages and disadvantages of integrating their warfighting operations in combat, and the legal and operational ramifications of such integrated combat operations. The paper concludes that integrated combat operations between the CIA and SOF are an appropriate template for warfare in certain situations, provided we develop and adhere to clear, well-understood criteria to manage this CIA-SOF warfighting relationship.

The war against terrorism is a fight for the preservation of our national interests and values, our way of life, and the very future of our country. We must employ every element of national power -- all necessary means -- in its prosecution. While managing the CIA-SOF warfighting relationship will present significant challenges, those challenges can be minimized in a manner that both preserves the combatant commander's flexibility and capitalizes on each agency's strengths and capabilities.

TABLE OF CONTENTS

PREFACE

This paper is dedicated to Judge Advocates everywhere who toil industriously but unremarked in loyal support and defense of our country and the rule of law.

"ALL NECESSARY MEANS" - EMPLOYING CIA OPERATIVES IN A WARFIGHTING ROLE ALONGSIDE SPECIAL OPERATIONS FORCES

> I wish to be useful, and every kind of service necessary to the public good becomes honorable by being necessary.

—Nathan Hale

This research paper looks at the separate roles, missions, and responsibilities of Central Intelligence Agency (CIA) paramilitary operatives and the Department of Defense (DOD) Special Operations Forces (SOF); the new and apparently *ad hoc* policy of integrating their operations together in combat; and the legal ramifications of such warfighting integration. This paper will be based on open source materials and media accounts of the CIA's involvement in the war against terrorism. This paper is intended as a general discussion vehicle for those legal issues associated with the employment of CIA paramilitary operatives in a warfighting role alongside SOF, and does not purport to speak with any operational authority regarding the conduct of CIA activities; nor does it discuss the wide range of traditional CIA activities that might be involved in the war against terrorism.

On September 11, 1999, a small number of operatives from the CIA were in Afghanistan. They were there in a non-combat mode for the purpose of recruiting sources, supporting anti-Taliban warlords and their operations, liaising with members of the Northern Alliance,[1] and generating intelligence on Osama bin Laden[2] and his Al Qaeda[3] terrorist organization.[4]

Two years later, on September 11, 2001, the United States was attacked by terrorist hijackers who flew three airliners into both towers of the World Trade Center in New York City, and the Pentagon in Washington, D.C. A fourth hijacked airliner, heading in the direction of Washington, D.C., crashed instead in a rural section of Pennsylvania.[5] These terrorist acts[6] killed over 3000 people and caused an estimated national economic loss of over $ 33 billion.[7] The evidence soon concluded that these acts of terrorism -- which amounted to an act of war[8] -- were committed by members of the terrorist organization known as Al Qaeda, and masterminded by Osama bin Laden.

On September 14, 2001, the United States Congress passed a joint resolution authorizing the President of the United States, George W. Bush, to "use all necessary and appropriate force" against those who were involved in the terrorist attacks that occurred against the U.S. on

September 11, 2001.[9] Close in time, President Bush signed a Memorandum of Notification[*] ordering the CIA to "use all necessary means" to destroy bin Laden and Al Qaeda.[10]

Consequently, CIA paramilitary teams were on the ground in Afghanistan "within days" of the attacks on New York and the Pentagon, "trained not just to observe conditions but if need be to change them," according to the CIA Deputy Director for Operations.[11] President Bush's Finding ordering the CIA to "use all necessary means" to destroy bin Laden and Al Qaeda meant the inserted CIA officers were legally free to identify Taliban and Al Qaeda targets for the Northern Alliance to attack; to accompany Northern Alliance and U.S. SOF units (when they arrived) on their combat missions against the Taliban; and to call in U.S. airstrikes against the Taliban and Al Qaeda.[12]

On September 24, 2001, a few days after the Presidential Finding, President Bush, acting pursuant to his Constitutional authority to conduct U.S. foreign relations and as Commander-in-Chief and Chief Executive, ordered the deployment of various combat equipped and combat support forces to several foreign nations in the Central and Pacific command areas of operations in order to prevent and deter further acts of terrorism.[13] Two weeks later, on October 7, 2001, President Bush announced that he had ordered the U.S. military to begin strikes against Al Qaeda terrorist training camps and Taliban[14] military installations in Afghanistan in order to disrupt the use of Afghanistan as a terrorist base of operations and to attack the military capability of the Taliban regime.[15]

CIA paramilitary operatives entered Afghanistan on 26 September 2001[16] ahead of U.S. Special Operations Forces (SOF) in order to link up with Northern Alliance[17] forces, secure helicopter landing zones for follow-on SOF, and guide SOF teams -- who arrived with their arsenal of laser target designators to enable U.S. aircraft to strike Taliban positions -- to the enemy.[18] These CIA officers were inserted ahead of the SOF because of their ability to get on the ground quickly, their language skills and knowledge of the terrain, and their existing contacts with anti-Taliban groups.[19] At the same time, U.S. military forces continued to flow quickly into Afghanistan, Uzbekistan, Pakistan, and the Arabian Sea, while the CIA continued to increase its activity in the region, adding logistics hubs, communication sites, and command and control centers and capabilities. All of this CIA paramilitary activity -- identifying targets, accompanying the Northern Alliance and SOF into combat, calling in airstrikes -- amounts to a warfighting role in the war against terrorism that continues today.

---

[*] Commonly known as a Presidential Finding.

CURRENT UNITED STATES POLICY

OBJECTIVE (ENDS)

The President's strategic objective is to win the global war on terrorism by employing all instruments of national power at his command, not just military power: "We will direct every resource at our command - every means of diplomacy, every tool of intelligence, every instrument of law enforcement, every financial influence and every necessary weapon of war - to the disruption and to the defeat of the global terror network."[20] The important point about the President's objective ("end") is that the war on terrorism is global in nature and directs multiple elements of U.S. national power against all terrorists who threaten U.S. interests; the war is not just about the destruction or capture of Al Qaeda.[21] This integration of all elements of national power is also one of the unifying themes of the 2002 National Military Strategy (pre-decisional draft) – to integrate military activities and operations with activities across the interagency spectrum.[22]

WAYS

Although CIA operatives have worked with U.S. military forces in the past,[23] their current warfighting operations in Afghanistan constitute the Agency's "most sweeping and lethal" covert action since its statutory founding in 1947 and signal a major return to the Agency's paramilitary involvement in armed conflicts.[24] This new policy, or course of action -- using CIA paramilitary operatives in a warfighting role alongside SOF (e.g., calling in airstrikes, accompanying SOF and Northern Alliance groups on combat missions, and other clandestine combat operations) -- epitomizes the President's determination to win the war on terrorism using all elements of national power, and constitutes "unprecedented" coordination between the CIA and SOF military units.[25]

According to Bob Woodward of the Washington Post, administration officials have said that President Bush has "pledged to dispatch military units to take advantage of the CIA's latest and best intelligence."[26] For example, according to one reporter, Dana Priest, Washington Post Staff Writer, it took just 316 SOF soldiers* to oust the Taliban from power, with nearly every A-team including one or two CIA operatives.[27] Priest even describes a mission briefing given by a CIA operative to both CIA and SOF personnel.[28] Other U.S. sources have said that SOF have been "seconded" to the CIA for paramilitary operations in Afghanistan.[29] In his book, Bush at War, Bob Woodward quotes the Chairman of the Joint Chiefs of Staff, General Richard B.

---

*Eighteen A-teams, four company-level units and three battalion-level commands, all reporting to a Joint Special Operations Task Force in Karshi, Uzbekistan, 100 miles north of the Afghanistan border.

Myers, as telling President Bush, "We're ready to put Special Forces on the ground with CIA forces."[30] Woodward also quotes "Hank," the CIA's counterterrorism special operations chief, as saying in a message to CIA assets in the field that, among other things, "we are fighting for the future of CIA/DOD integrated counterterrorism warfare around the globe . . . [w]hile we will make mistakes as we chart new territory and new methodology, our objectives are clear, and our concept of partnership is sound."[31]

Regardless of who is seconded to whom, however, it is clear that the war in Afghanistan highlights not just the tight integration, but also the erosion of distinctions between SOF and the CIA in the war against terrorism. Past administrations made more of an effort to differentiate between military combat activities and CIA missions.[32] In the war on terrorism, however, the Bush Administration has gradually blurred these distinctive lines in response to an asymmetrical, non-State threat that requires greater coordination and cooperation among intelligence, military, and law enforcement officials.[33]

RESOURCES/MEANS

To accomplish his strategic objective and resource this course of action, President Bush ordered the use of all necessary means.[34] This order in turn generated an operationally-driven *ad hoc* relationship between CIA paramilitary operatives and SOF on the ground in Afghanistan that resulted in improved lethality and agility on the battlefield stemming from each group's distinct contribution to warfighting. For example, Jim Pavitt, head of the CIA's clandestine service, acknowledged publicly in a speech that the CIA's covert operations inside Afghanistan immediately after September 11 paved the way for follow-on SOF and the resulting rout of the Taliban in the fall of 2001.[35] Clearly then, working together, the CIA's and SOF's respective capabilities complimented each other in a manner sufficient to ensure the defeat of the Taliban. According to one author, this new type of operation involving "fastmoving CIA paramilitary teams" and SOF may well "serve as a model for future encounters against terrorism in other parts of the world . . . [t]he dramatic success of specialized use of reconnaissance weapons and a dynamic, small-unit combat strategy obviated" the need to deploy large numbers of ground troops.[36]

Clearly, the full spectrum dominance bought with this CIA-SOF integration of warfighting capabilities has produced a new, successful battlefield synergy. Improving the _ways_ of warfighting by integrating all _means_ has resulted in a synergy that has not only succeeded, but that has transformed the traditional view on the prosecution of armed conflict.

RISKS

This multidimensional integration is not without significant legal and operational risks, however. The CIA and SOF communities possess very distinct identities and mandates, with separate legal authorities, operating structures, and methods of organization. Though this relationship between the DOD and CIA has been successful to date, and was praised by Secretary of Defense Donald Rumsfeld (who was also Secretary of Defense in the mid-1970s) in February 2002 as "good as I've ever seen it . . . They've got a darn good record . . . ,"[37] the relationship has not been without problems that deserve attention. To understand the context of these problems and their associated issues, however, this paper must first review the statutory basis, and roles and missions, of the DOD, SOF and the CIA.

DOD AND CIA AUTHORITIES AND MISSIONS

Separate groups of Constitutional authorities, statutory authorities and responsibilities, and executive orders separate the CIA and DOD/SOF, which in turn delineate separate divisions of responsibility for national security.

DEPARTMENT OF DEFENSE

Legal Authority

Constitutional. The legal authority for the existence of the armed forces is set forth in Articles I and II of the U.S. Constitution. Specifically, Article I, Section 8, provides that the Congress shall have the power to raise and support Armies, to provide and maintain a Navy, and to make rules for the government and regulation of the same. Article II, Section 2, provides that the President shall be Commander-in-Chief of the Army and Navy of the United States.[38]

Statutory (U.S. Code). While the U.S. Constitution provides the overarching genesis of authority for the armed forces, Title 10 of the United States Code fills in the blanks by codifying in more concrete terms the statutory authority, and broad missions and functions, of DOD.[39]

Roles and Missions

DOD Writ Large. Of more practical daily use is the delineation of DOD's mission statement in DOD Directive 5100.1, *Functions of the Department of Defense and its Major Components.* Specifically, as prescribed by higher authority (*i.e.*, U.S. Code Title 10), the DOD "shall maintain and employ Armed Forces to: Support and defend the Constitution of the United States against all enemies, foreign and domestic; ensure, by timely and effective *military action* (emphasis added by author), the security of the United States, its possessions, and areas vital to its interests; and uphold and advance the national policies and interests of the United States.[40]

SOF. Wartime special operations conducted by U.S. armed forces are as old as the American Revolutionary War, in which General George Washington approved a plan for several of his soldiers to capture the traitor Benedict Arnold and return him to American control.[41] In 1986, as part of the Goldwater-Nichols Department of Defense Reorganization Act,[42] Congress consolidated all SOF from all the services into one new command, the U.S. Special Operations Command. This reorganization resulted in large part from the failed 1980 Desert One operation to rescue American hostages in Iran, which exposed shortfalls in the training and equipping of SOF and highlighted in tragic form the neglect that the covert side of warfare had suffered for far too long.[43]

SOF forces conduct special operations missions and activities in war and peace, either independent from or integrated with conventional military operations.[44] While special operations encompass the use of small units in direct or indirect military actions, they are usually focused on strategic and operational objectives, which are frequently shaped by political-military considerations, thereby requiring "clandestine, covert, or low-visibility techniques and oversight at the national level."[45] SOF units consist of combinations of specialized personnel, training, equipment, and tactics that exceed the routine capabilities of conventional military forces.[46] Importantly, unless otherwise directed by the President or Secretary of Defense, a special operations activity or mission is supposed to ["shall"] be conducted under the command of the unified combatant commander[47] in whose geographic area the activity or mission is to be conducted.[48] Secretary of Defense Donald Rumsfeld's recent change establishing the U.S. Special Operations Command as both a *supported* and *supporting* command may require a change to Title 10 of the U.S. Code.

The current National Military Strategy of the United States provides that the Armed Forces "are the Nation's instrument for ensuring our security," their primary purpose is to "defeat" threats of violence against the U.S. should deterrence fail, and their foremost task is to "fight and win our Nation's wars."[49] The Pre-Decisional Draft of the 2002 National Military Strategy of the United States of America, dated 19 September 2002, continues the theme of the previous strategy by stating that our national military objectives remain, among other things, to "defend the Nation" and "win the Nation's wars."[50] However, the Constitution does not dictate how (ways) our country should be protected, or what our national security establishment should specifically look like. This flexibility in national defense has produced various statutory and regulatory forms of national security organization, to include the National Security Act of 1947,[51] which is codified in portions of Titles 10, 32 and 50 of the United States Code.

CENTRAL INTELLIGENCE AGENCY

Legal Authority

Statutory (U.S. Code). The legal basis for the CIA is set forth in the National Security Act of 1947, which established the CIA and the DOD, among other agencies.[52]

Constitutional. Intelligence operations are as old as our Nation, as noted in the 64th Federalist, which "commended" the new U.S. Constitution, in granting power to the President to make treaties, for providing the <u>means</u> (resources) "by which the President could 'manage the business of intelligence in such a manner as prudence may suggest."[63]

Roles and Missions

Definition of Covert Action. One of the CIA's several missions, among other duties and responsibilities related to intelligence functions, is to conduct <u>special activities</u> approved by the President.[54] Special Activities were defined by President Reagan in Executive Order 12333, United States Intelligence Activities, dated December 4, 1981, and still in effect, as "activities conducted in support of national foreign policy objectives abroad which are planned and executed so that the role of the United States Government is not apparent or acknowledged publicly."[55] In fact, no agency except the CIA may conduct any special activity unless the President directs such, and the CIA itself must have a Presidential Finding in order to conduct special activities or covert action.[56] The U.S. military may also conduct special activities during a time of war declared by Congress or during any period covered by a report from the President to the Congress under the War Powers Resolution.[57]

According to one author, Executive Order 12333's reference to "special activities" is a euphemism for "covert action."[58] In fact, 10 years later, in the Intelligence Authorization Act of 1991, Congress provided a detailed definition of covert action that closely resembles the definition of "special activities" in Executive Order 12333, specifically: an "activity or activities of the United States Government to influence political, economic, or military conditions abroad, where it is intended that the role of the United States Government will not be apparent or acknowledged publicly, but does not include . . . traditional . . . military activities or routine support to such activities."[69] This language -- the definition of covert action in the 1991 Intelligence Authorization Act -- is mirrored in Title 50, U.S. Code, Section 413b(e)[60]and remains the controlling legal definition for covert action today, even though Executive Order 12333 -- and its definition of "special activities" -- remains effective as well.

In plain language, then, covert action is action designed to produce certain results in foreign countries without such action being clearly and openly identified with the United States. Accordingly, because it can be a convenient and stealthy tool for the execution of foreign policy, covert action has been the traditional tool of U.S. Presidents when confronted with problems that have not responded to other tools of statecraft pressure.[61] Former Director of Central Intelligence Stansfield Turner explained it best when he stated, "Covert action is not intelligence. Covert action is the conduct of foreign policy. Its object is to affect the course of events, not to inform our policy makers about events."[62] Further, the most extreme form of covert action -- paramilitary operations -- can be described as secret wars, according to David Isenberg, a research associate at the Washington-based Cato Institute Project on Military Procurement.[63]

Legal Authority for Covert Action. Interestingly, the National Security Act of 1947 did not explicitly indicate that the CIA as an agency should or would engage in covert action, nor did it specify therein that covert action is one of the CIA's assigned missions.[64] In fact, nowhere in the Act was covert action mentioned, although some have argued that the Act's legislative history indicates an intention for the CIA to collect intelligence by engaging in espionage (vice covert action) abroad.[65]

Accordingly, the CIA's covert action mission, and underlying capability attendant thereto, have an ambiguous foundation. Nevertheless, successive Presidential administrations have found statutory authority for the CIA to conduct covert action in an obscure phrase in the agency's basic charter, wherein the "CIA is given the duty 'to perform such other functions and duties related to intelligence affecting the national security as the National Security Council may from time to time direct.'"[66] The U.S. Congress "acquiesced" in this interpretation;[67] and early National Security Council directives during the Cold War instructed the CIA to conduct paramilitary operations as part of the U.S. effort to contain the former Soviet Union.[68] During the 1950's, "more and more covert operations were assigned to the CIA because State and Defense did not want to do them in the open or because the simplest and fastest way to get something done was to assign the job to the secret arm."[69]

Interestingly, the CIA's first general counsel, Lawrence R. Houston, who helped draft the Act establishing the CIA, has stated that the clause permitting the CIA to engage in "such other functions" referred only to intelligence collection and not to covert action, and that the CIA was stretching the law's original intent by using the "such other functions" clause to justify covert action.[70] According to Houston, "all during this drafting of the Act, all during the presentations to congressional committees, there was no mention of covert action. . . It was entirely intelligence . . . That was [to be] the sole product."[71] After the Act was passed into law, however, and at the request of Truman administration officials, Houston wrote a legal opinion stating that the CIA could legally execute covert action if the President gave it a directive to do so and if Congress funded the action.[72]

Thus began the dawn of CIA covert actions, and U.S. Presidents have "systematically employed [the CIA] as a mechanism through which they can . . . carry out military actions (emphasis added) without the armed forces."[73] The Intelligence Authorization Act of 1991, codified in Title 50, U.S. Code, Section 413 and discussed above, further solidified in statute the definition of, and authority to conduct, covert action. One type of covert action that closely resembles military action is the CIA's paramilitary operations, or, according to one author, "unconventional warfare: to support or stimulate armed resistance elements in their homeland against the regime in power, or to employ irregular troops to invade a country and unseat its regime – or a combination of both."[74] The President may not authorize the conduct of a covert action, however, unless he determines such an action is necessary to support identifiable foreign policy objectives of the United States and is important to the national security of the United States. That determination must be set forth in a written finding.[75] Further, each finding must specify each agency or other U.S. Government entity that is authorized to fund or otherwise participate in any significant way in such covert action,[76] and no finding may authorize any action that would violate the Constitution or any statute of the United States.[77]

CIA Support to Military Operations. While America's history of covert action dates back to the colonial era, when Revolutionary officials conspired with certain Bermuda officials to "obtain" a store of gunpowder from the Royal Arsenal at Bermuda,[78] the "CIA's" history of support to U.S. military operations is also not new, but began immediately upon the birth of the CIA's predecessor agency.

"CIA" support to military operations originated during World War II, with the creation of the Office of Strategic Services (OSS), which built for its own use a covert paramilitary force.[79] OSS officers ran commando operations in Europe, acted as guides in the Allied landings in North Africa in 1942, conducted sabotage to support the Allied landings in Normandy in 1944, established effective intelligence sources and networks, provided technical and logistical support to resistance groups and fighters, and worked to coordinate paramilitary activities with conventional military operations.[80] Of note is the fact that OSS agents also received instructions from military commanders, and "reported on the results of sabotage missions and the effectiveness of Allied bombing."[81] According to Charles D. Ameringer in his book, U.S. Foreign

<u>Intelligence - The Secret Side of American History</u>, OSS field activities were under the control of the theater commanders.[82]

CIA paramilitary operatives continued to operate with U.S. military forces in Korea, Vietnam, and the Gulf War, and in recent years the Agency has actually been tasked to provide direct support to military operations and deployments.[83] With the exponential growth in U.S. military peacekeeping deployments in the 1990s, there was a concomitant need by the Armed Forces for ever more tactical intelligence support, and President William Clinton supported that need by issuing a 1995 Presidential Order (Presidential Decision Directive (PDD) - 35) instructing the Intelligence Community to provide the military with the tactical intelligence it needed.[84] During a visit to CIA headquarters a few months after issuing PDD-35, President Clinton explained his directive and emphasized that the intelligence community's "first priority was to support 'the intelligence needs of our military during an operation,' and that commanders in the field needed 'prompt, thorough intelligence to fully inform their decisions and maximize the security of our troops.'"[85]

According to CIA officials, however, this resulted in a "diversion of shrinking national *strategic* (emphasis added) intelligence resources to growing, *tactical* (emphasis added) missions.'[86] Despite other warnings from intelligence community officials that DOD budgetary cuts were forcing the armed forces to "trim [their] tactical intelligence programs" and thereby shift their work to the "national" intelligence services, Congress did not resist this "shift of national means to tactical ends.'[87] Whether this is a smart move in the long run is not within the scope of this paper. However, as will be discussed later in this paper, U.S. Central Command is successfully fighting the war against terrorism by using the CIA, a national strategic resource (means), in an operational/tactical-level warfight (ways) in order to achieve both the President's strategic objective (win the war on terrorism) and the operational-level objective (disrupt the use of Afghanistan as a safe haven for terrorists and destroy the military capability of the Taliban and Al Qaeda).

COVERT ACTION WITHIN DOD

Integrated CIA-SOF combat operations in support of Operation Enduring Freedom have transcended the typical forms of unconventional warfare performed by each agency and have even been described as a new template for warfare. Despite the successful resurgence of CIA paramilitary covert action in the war against terrorism in Afghanistan, however, one CIA veteran has told Bob Woodward of the Washington Post that the CIA is "not fully equipped or trained" to perform the high-risk operations that President Bush directed in his Presidential Finding ordering the CIA to "destroy bin Laden and Al Qaeda," since the Directorate of Operations, which runs covert actions, "has been out of the business of funding and managing lethal covert action" since the end of the Cold War.[88] This opinion, although certainly not dispositive, is not new. Back in 1987, Allan E. Goodman, relying on former CIA Director Stansfield Turner's contention that a majority of espionage professionals believe that covert activities detract from the CIA's primary mission to collect and analyze intelligence, proposed that covert action should be limited to paramilitary operations and given to the Department of Defense.[89] Even earlier, in 1975, Harry Rositzke championed the transfer of paramilitary covert action (a subset of covert action) to the Department of Defense based on his belief that the "self-defeating amalgam of covert action and secret intelligence in one organization was key to the CIA's ineffectiveness.[90] It would seem that the CIA has never seen a time in its history when someone has not been declaring the ineffectiveness of its covert actions, as many others over the years have also called for the transfer of paramilitary covert actions to the Department of Defense.

Rositzke's proposal to transfer the CIA's paramilitary operations to DOD makes somewhat more sense than Goodman's proposal to limit all covert action to paramilitary covert action and also transfer such to DOD. By limiting covert action to only paramilitary action, Goodman's proposal would remove from the CIA's arsenal those non-paramilitary intelligence tools that are not appropriate for DOD or any other government agency to execute, such as influence operations, press placements, exfiltration operations, etc. Limiting covert activities to paramilitary operations would also severely restrict the President's ability to conduct effective foreign policy. In addition, the transfer of covert paramilitary operations to DOD would confront the military with an operational problem for which it has no prior history – *i.e.*, the possibility that a military operation would have to be undertaken in the context of official deniability. If the covert military operation was of vital interest to U.S. security but also extremely sensitive, the President would be vulnerable to the unfortunate possibility that one day he might have to choose between abandoning military personnel in the field in order to maintain plausible deniability, or acknowledging the covert activity, with all the second and third order affects attendant thereto.

This leads to another issue. The use of formal military force to conduct a covert military operation amounts to an act of war in terms of international law. If such an operation were undertaken and was somehow discovered and publicized, the President would not only lack plausible deniability, but unless he was prepared to punish severely the military personnel involved (which would be extremely difficult to do if he directed or "permitted" the operation), the Nation would face *de facto* and *de jure* a condition of war that had not been authorized by

Congress. By using the CIA, or some other non-military organization to undertake such missions, the President at least fuzzes the legal issue of an act of war. While it is true that CIA covert actions can themselves amount to an act of war, the President can use the CIA to engage in an act of war without U.S. fingerprints. This capability lies in the CIA's lap for a reason.

The following example is illustrative and assists our analysis here. U.S. intelligence sources discover an Al Qaeda command and control headquarters in a friendly country, and the President decides it must be destroyed. If responsibility for paramilitary covert action were to lie with the Department of Defense, then the President would direct the Secretary of Defense to conduct a deniable <u>covert</u> operation to destroy the terrorist headquarters. Technically, the Department of Defense could execute the mission with minimal difficulty. SOF possess the required skill-sets and would need only to render anonymous their fingerprints: no uniforms or other identification tags associated with the U.S., and no weapons traceable back to the U.S. Operationally, however, several roadblocks present themselves.

By entering the friendly country with military forces in execution of a military mission, the U.S. has committed an act of war even though our interest lies not with them but in the terrorist headquarters. [Note: This is so regardless of whether the mission is executed by SOF in a covert mode or in a public mode, or whether it is executed by CIA paramilitary operatives, for that matter]. The Secretary of Defense's tasking to U.S. Special Operations Command to execute this covert action ("act of war"), however, works smoothly only if we can get SOF into and out of Pakistan without their being noticed. In that case, we have a *de facto* war that is deniable. If any of the SOF are captured or killed, however, we have a *de jure* act of war. Most of the world has come to look at CIA *de facto* wars as a way of life because most powers benefit from their own CIA-equivalents operating in foreign countries, with nothing to be gained politically by claiming an act of war when another's covert action is discovered. The world, however, is not likely to tolerate the U.S. throwing its regular military muscle around in a covert fashion. The world will rightly ask: Where does it stop? If the U.S. employs SOF to conduct deniable covert action, then is the next step a clandestine tomahawk missile strike, or maybe even a missile strike whose origin is manipulated to conceal U.S. fingerprints?

By abdicating their open identification as U.S. military personnel, SOF would forfeit their Geneva Conventions status. This is important not just because of their loss of entitlement to prisoner of war status should they be captured, but also because of their loss of lawful combatant immunity against charges of spying, or murder for anyone they killed in the operation. SOF in this scenario could also be considered unlawful combatants.

There is another consequence if SOF forfeit their U.S. identity in a covert military operation. If they are killed, the lack of evidence associating them with the U.S. would preserve the President's plausible deniability option, and the dead SOF personnel would not be affected because they are, after all, dead. If SOF are captured, however, the issue is more difficult. The President could continue to plausibly deny the operation in spite of claims by the captives that they are U.S. military personnel, although such claims would undoubtedly muddy the political waters, create a public relations challenge, and embarrass the President. The more significant aspect to the President's decision to continue denying the operation would be that the SOF captives could expect to receive no protection or help from the U.S. If the CIA were to conduct the operation, however, these issues disappear because CIA paramilitary operatives are trained -- from their first day in that specialty -- to accept as part of their mission the requirement to operate in the "cold," without protection or help from their Government.

It is unlikely that the Secretary of Defense or anyone else could lawfully order SOF personnel to conduct a covert action that would require them to forfeit their Geneva Convention status in order to retain deniability. Clearly a commander could issue a lawful order to SOF to conduct a covert operation, but no one can order military personnel to forfeit their status as otherwise lawful combatants in the execution of that mission. This is problematic. Covert actions are not covert if they lose their anonymity and deniability. SOF personnel, however, although permitted to reduce their operating profile like any good soldier, can be required only to maintain the secrecy of their mission, not to actively hide their military identity to their detriment. Accordingly, the Department of Defense would be seriously limited in its ability to execute successful covert military operations that are anonymous and deniable. This dilemma could be solved if there is found within the SOF ranks a sufficient number willing to forfeit this status. The method used to solicit such "volunteers," however, is fraught with the dangers of undue influence, peer pressure, traditional military values, the U.S. public's long-standing expectations of how their SOF sons and daughters will be treated at the hands of the enemy, and, perhaps most important, informed consent.

Lastly, some form of legal instrument would likely be needed to empower and direct the Department of Defense to conduct the type and scope of covert actions heretofore conducted under the CIA's domain. Regardless of the necessary legal mechanism, however, the issues discussed above highlight the complications associated with tasking the Department of Defense to conduct covert actions. In the 2004 defense budget Secretary of Defense Donald Rumsfeld provided the U.S. Special Operations Command with more budget authority and manpower to enable it to assume an expanded strategic military role. Recent press reports have speculated

13

that this new role will include covert actions similar to the CIA's. If this is so, this change in roles and missions for SOF should be approached with great caution and informed analysis.

LEGAL RAMIFICATIONS OF INTEGRATED CIA-SOF WARFIGHTING

There are a number of profound legal and operational issues associated with integrating CIA and SOF warfighting operations, and then managing that integrated relationship on the battlefield. This remains so whether the operation is CIA-led, with SOF seconded to the Agency, or vice versa, with SOF in the lead and CIA seconded. These issues are categorized in the following discussion under the general subheadings of Deniability, Lawful Action, Geneva Conventions, and Command and Control. As these issues are discussed below, it is important to keep in mind that in integrated CIA-SOF warfighting, SOF are still conducting military operations. The CIA paramilitary operatives are usually also performing military operations. Further, although the CIA paramilitary operatives maintain their covert cover, SOF hide only the mission and not their U.S. identity, although they have every right to reduce their profile through lawful means. A collateral effect during integrated operations is that SOF often become the CIA paramilitaries' operational cover.

DENIABILITY

While some covert CIA operations receive extensive support from various military units and DOD agencies, in general the intent is for the CIA's covert operations -- because of their very purpose and nature -- to avoid overly close identification with the U.S. Government.[91] Nevertheless, the more often we integrate CIA and SOF operations on the battlefield, the more we subject the covert action to an overly close identification with the U.S. Government, with resultant "deniability" problems. In contrast, stand-alone SOF operations demonstrate a public commitment of U.S. military forces to protect our national interests, though the specifics may remain secret or receive little scrutiny. Such secrecy, however, at times provides SOF the opportunity to operate closer to the edge of the law.[92]

"Paramilitary operations are the noisiest of all covert actions."[93] Add to that noise the presence of U.S. military forces alongside CIA paramilitary operatives, and one runs the risk of making the covert action more visible to its enemies. As the size of the operation increases, secrecy becomes more problematic, particularly if military or paramilitary forces are involved. Forces mean people, and people talk.[94] As the size of the operation increases, it also becomes more complicated, with the attendant possibility that something will go wrong. For example, the end of the covert Iran-Contra operation began when a "single American survived an airplane crash."[95]

14

LAWFUL ACTION

Another issue associated with integrated CIA-SOF warfighting operations is the lawfulness of each agency's methods of operations. CIA covert paramilitary operations may be contrary to customary international law or the laws of the country in which the activity is taking place, whereas U.S. military forces routinely operate in the public domain in a legally based forum requiring them to follow international law, with all the attendant scrutiny and Monday-morning second-guessing. When the CIA and SOF operate together on the battlefield, the legal distinctions regarding operating authorities and procedures, and accountability, can become blurred. While these blurred boundaries are of significant concern, they can be overcome through situational awareness and adherence to proper governing (legal) authorities.

Given that some rogue countries and non-State entities such as Al Qaeda and other terrorist groups have threatened the United States and its allies and friends with death and destruction, the U.S. must be prepared to take whatever action it deems necessary in order to protect our vital interests.[96] Nevertheless, the employment of the CIA and DOD in protecting such interests must be consistent with national law. Whereas U.S. military operations are more easily proven to be in compliance with both national and international law because they occur in the public domain, this is not the case with CIA covert operations.[97] Covert actions do not imply that U.S. law is superior to that of another country's, or that of international law, but that, instead, there are overriding national interests (vital interests) that must be protected outside the framework of international law and regular diplomatic relations.[98]

While there is a statutory requirement for CIA covert actions to comply with U.S. national law,[99] there is no parallel statutory requirement for such actions to comply with international law. According to Ronald Kessler in Inside the CIA - Revealing the Secrets of the World's Most Powerful Spy Agency, it is the job of the Directorate of Operations (the CIA Directorate that undertakes covert action) to "break the laws of other countries."[100] Stansfield Turner, CIA Director during the Carter Administration, stated in 1996, when comparing the CIA to the FBI, a law enforcement agency, that "The FBI agent's first reaction when given a job is, 'How do I do this within the law?'," whereas the CIA agent's first reaction when given a mission is, "How do I do this regardless of the law of the country in which I am operating?"[101] When William Webster became Director of the CIA after the Iran-Contra affair, however, he reemphasized the need to ensure CIA activities complied at a minimum with U.S. national law, if not international law. One of his policy imperatives was to make sure that every proposal from the White House and National Security Council not only made sense, but also complied with established U.S. law and precedent. He did this by testing every covert action proposal "against a set of unvarying

15

questions: Does it fall within U.S. law? What would happen if it became public? Will the public understand it? Finally, will it work?"[102]

The DOD, on the other hand, is legally bound to execute its military operations in accordance not only with national law but also the international treaties governing the laws of armed conflict to which the U.S. is a signatory. Further, U.S. government policy dictates that U.S. military forces must "comply with the law of war during all armed conflicts, however such conflicts are characterized, and with the principles and spirit of the law of war during all other operations."[103] This policy edict is important for two reasons: First, the laws of war generally apply only to international armed conflicts between nation-states (and organized resistance movements under certain circumstances);[104] second, the laws of war usually do not govern the conduct of military personnel against non-State actors in law enforcement operations.[105] Thus, even though the U.S.-led war against terrorism is not an international armed conflict between nation-states, U.S. military forces must adhere to the international laws of war as codified in the various Geneva and Hague Conventions.

The CIA, however, is under no similar requirement regarding international law. This provides the U.S. with tremendous flexibility when it implements foreign policy. Because of the additional legal constraints imposed on the DOD, however, we must be careful to maintain a well-delineated separation between the CIA and DOD when they integrate their battlefield operations.

Accountability and control of CIA paramilitary covert actions on the battlefield are just as vital as they are for SOF operations if all such activities are to remain legitimate instruments of U.S. foreign policy. Accountability and control demonstrate that regardless of the mixture of CIA-SOF forces on the battlefield, their integrated operations are compatible with our democratic form of government because they are conducted with accountability and adherence to the law.[106] For CIA covert activities to remain a viable option in furtherance of our national security, they must also have the support of the American people in overarching concept, if not the details. In this regard, the CIA is ultimately accountable to the American people -- whether directly, or through the Congress.[107]

This accountability and control are assured because, as discussed previously, the U.S. Code mandates that covert actions not be contrary to the U.S. Constitution or our Nation's laws.[108] This also means that CIA operatives remain subject to international norms, human rights laws, and war crimes prosecutions, should they get themselves into that situation.[109] This accountability is further ensured in that, as noted earlier, CIA covert actions must be authorized by the President, and the Agency must report to the House and Senate Intelligence committees for accountability and oversight purposes.[110]

GENEVA CONVENTIONS

During the U.S. Civil War, the Lincoln Administration commissioned Francis Lieber, a professor at Columbia College, to draft a code of the laws of war, which became the basis of The Hague and Geneva Conventions, to which the United States is a signatory.[111] In 1863 Mr. Lieber advised President Lincoln and the Union Army that guerrillas, spies, and saboteurs could be summarily shot.[112]

Because CIA personnel operate without uniforms or identification as U.S. Government officers -- even though their arsenal includes airplanes, helicopters, and unmanned aerial Predators armed with Hellfire missiles, all typically thought of as military equipment -- they are not normally afforded the protections of the Geneva Conventions, whereas regular military forces are. In a combat operation where CIA and SOF forces are tightly integrated, the result could be that, if captured, the SOF soldiers are afforded Geneva Convention protections while the CIA operatives are not; further, CIA operatives might even be considered by the enemy to be unlawful combatants. Worse, the intermingling of CIA and SOF forces/operations could result in our enemy, unable to distinguish between the two groups, categorizing all captives as unlawful combatants.

While this lack of lawful combatant status is a condition that CIA paramilitary operatives work under daily, such is not the case for U.S. military personnel. Further, from a practical standpoint, should such a dilemma arise, would U.S. officials be willing to stand up and say, "the SOF captives are prisoners of war entitled to Geneva Convention protections, but the CIA operatives you are holding captive are not"? Are U.S. officials equipped with such moral courage? How would the American public react to such a statement, even if they knew the officials spoke the truth about the status of the CIA captives? Additionally, how would we explain the presence of CIA operatives with military forces but, more importantly, if we decide to officially acknowledge their presence on the battlefield, how would we categorize their status: lawful combatants (even if they are not wearing uniforms or distinctive insignia)? Noncombatants? Entitled to Geneva Conventions protections? There may be no good answers to these questions when we must resort to protecting our national interests through CIA paramilitary operations.

In some conflicts, such as the current war against terrorism, the issue of whether Geneva Convention status applies to SOF but not to CIA operatives may be irrelevant in law, though not irrelevant in diplomatic relations and on the political stage. As noted earlier, the laws of war generally apply only to international armed conflicts between nation-states (and organized resistance movements under certain circumstances).[113] This means that the Geneva Conventions apply normally when *nations* fight. So, if members of an integrated CIA-SOF team are captured by a *State* actor (*e.g.*, a member of the Armed Forces of a hostile country) during an international armed conflict, the CIA operatives normally would not be entitled to prisoner of war/Geneva Conventions status, whereas the military team members would, so long as they do not meet one of the exceptions, such as acting as spies or saboteurs in hostile territory. If that same CIA-SOF team is captured by a *non-State* actor, such as a terrorist group, the military members are technically not prisoners of war but are instead crime victims – hostages, in fact, subject to immediate release under Geneva Convention III.[114] In such a case, the U.S. could legally demand that all of the captives, both CIA operatives and SOF, be immediately released. The U.S. could also argue on the stage of world opinion that all captives -- whether CIA or SOF -- should be treated by their non-State captors in accordance with the Geneva Conventions as a matter of policy, just as the U.S. does even when a conflict does not rise to the level of an international armed conflict. That argument is likely to fail, however, given the Bush Administration's decision to classify all Taliban and Al Qaeda fighters as unlawful combatants not entitled to prisoner of war status, although the Administration's policy is to treat them in a manner consistent with the principles of the Geneva Conventions.

COMMAND AND CONTROL

As a consequence of the Goldwater-Nichols Department of Defense Reorganization Act of 1986,[115] Unified Combatant Commanders[116] are charged with overseeing all military operations in their regional areas of responsibility, whether conducted by conventional military forces or SOF.[117] Title 10, U.S. Code, Section 162(a)(4) states with more specificity that, "except as otherwise directed by the Secretary of Defense, all forces operating within the geographic area assigned to a unified combatant command shall be assigned to, and under the command of, the commander of that command."[118] Further, a combatant commander is responsible to the President and to the Secretary of Defense for the performance of missions assigned to that command.[119] To implement this authority in military regulations, DOD Directive 5100.1, *Functions of the Department of Defense and Its Major Components,* assigns the combatant commanders with the command function to employ forces within that combatant command as he considers necessary to carry out missions assigned to the command.[120] Of additional note is the fact that commanders of commands and forces assigned to a combatant command are under the authority, direction, and control of, and are responsible to, the combatant commander on all matters for which the combatant commander has been assigned authority.[121]

Stated more succinctly, the combatant commander has the responsibility for missions in his geographical area of command, and commands all military forces assigned to his area of responsibility. The combatant commander, however, has no specific statutory authority over other U.S. Government personnel in his area of operations, such as CIA paramilitary operatives. Accordingly, when CIA paramilitary operatives are integrated with SOF in a warfighting operation in a combatant commander's area of operations, the combatant commander has no authority over those CIA paramilitary operatives -- whose very presence in that integrated mix is in furtherance of a military mission -- unless the President has given him such authority. This lack of authority over all participants in the combatant commander's military mission can potentially but not necessarily handicap the combatant commander's statutory responsibility to the President and Secretary of Defense to accomplish his assigned missions. Accordingly, this potential problem must be addressed up front in the planning stages of every military operation in which integrated CIA-SOF operations may be employed.

One way to resolve this potential problem would be to place CIA paramilitary assets directly under the authority and control of the regional combatant commanders. One journalist, Nathan Hodge of Defense Week, has opined that in wartime the CIA Director is "supposed to put all CIA assets within a given command region . . . under the operational control of the regional commander in chief" because the CIA is mainly an intelligence gathering agency, with military operations not one of its core, or traditional competencies.[122] Hodge reinforces his opinion on this matter with his assertion that when the CIA receives information of value to U.S. commanders, it should turn such information over to the "professional" [U.S. military] warfighters.[123] Hodge also asserts that even though officers from the CIA's predecessor agency, the Office of Strategic Services (OSS), worked under military commanders in World War II, the CIA in Afghanistan today is conducting its own campaign independent of U.S. Central Command. Hodge proposes that this is consistent with the CIA's pattern of "resisting subordination to military command," and he cites as examples the CIA's covert paramilitary actions in Honduras, Nicaragua, and El Salvador during the 1980s, where the CIA completely bypassed the Combatant Commander of U.S. Southern Command.[124] Hodge fails to note, however, that all such CIA operations are undertaken at the order of the President, the Commander-in-Chief.

Another opinion in a vein similar to that of Hodge's is that of Michael Vickers, a former Army Green Beret and CIA official and now the Director of Strategic Studies at the Center for

19

Strategic and Budgetary Assessments. According to a press report quoting Mr. Vickers, all of the CIA operatives in Afghanistan, including the operators of the Predator drones, are supposed to report to U.S. Central Command, but they also report to the CIA's Near-East Division, which is responsible for Afghanistan and Pakistan.[125] However, Vickers notes that not all CIA paramilitary operatives have diligently consulted with, much less reported to, their military commanders, leading to some friction.[126]

In an article written before and independent of Hodge's, Douglas Waller, writing for Time magazine, made some additional observations. According to Waller, after Vietnam and the scandals of the 1970s, the CIA practically disbanded its paramilitary force, and when they subsequently needed paramilitary experts for their own covert actions against the Soviets in Afghanistan or to train contra rebels in Nicaragua, the Agency "borrowed" Army Green Berets or Navy SEALs, or hired retired SOF on a contract basis. Waller also noted that, in the past two years, CIA Director George Tenet has expanded the CIA's paramilitary force to the point where, according to one intelligence source cited by Waller, "the CIA is practically creating its own army, navy and air force."[127]

Another way to resolve this potential problem (i.e., the combatant commander's lack of direct authority and control over CIA paramilitary operatives in his area of responsibility) is for the CIA paramilitary operatives to maintain their separate (CIA) line of authority but be required to coordinate and consult directly with the combatant commander when they will be part of an integrated CIA-SOF warfighting operation. This option is more practical and realistic in a large scale military operation such as the global war on terrorism. For example, it is working successfully in Afghanistan today, although on an *ad hoc* rather than a formalized (required coordination and consultation) basis. In his book Bush at War, Bob Woodward describes how "Hank," the CIA's counterterrorism special operations chief met with General Tommy Franks, commander of U.S. Central Command, and made it clear that the CIA paramilitary teams in Afghanistan would be "working for Franks," somewhat contrary to recent practice, as "partners" with the military.[128] This option will not only help to reduce the potential problem discussed above, but will preserve the combatant commander's operational flexibility to capitalize on the strengths that each agency (CIA and DOD/SOF) brings to the battlefield by applying the force most advantageous to successful mission accomplishment.

In further support of this option, CIA operatives are reportedly working "hand in glove" with SOF and have provided a "crucial eyes-on-the-ground capability," while still reporting through CIA operational channels.[129] CIA paramilitary operatives are small in number, flexible, and generally freer from bureaucratic hierarchies than their SOF counterparts, who must usually jump through 18 food chains, 20 levels of paperwork and 22 hoops before they can take action.[130] CIA operatives are able to use cash and other favors, such as supplying modern combat gear, to buy loyalty and information from tribal warlords in Afghanistan, whereas military forces do not possess such legal authorities.[131] Another advantage to using CIA paramilitary operatives is that their ability to pinpoint the enemy is in many cases more humane than a full-scale military assault because the result will generally be fewer civilian casualties.[132] In a war against terrorists, where the enemy does not wear uniforms and intermingles with the local populace, CIA paramilitary operatives are better able to distinguish the "good guys from the bad guys" and thus identify the right targets.[133]

Nevertheless, close cooperation and intermingling between the CIA and SOF is fraught with danger given their respective cultures, operational modes, sources of information, and oversight structures.[134] For example, the CIA did not always obtain landing rights from neighboring countries before it moved its teams into Afghanistan, and it was free to ignore the traditional military requirement when going into combat to be backed up with an extraction plan and search-and-rescue teams. If the CIA teams got into any trouble, they were on their own.[135]

Integrated CIA and SOF warfighting operations, accordingly, invite significant legal and operational issues associated with deniability, legality, Geneva Conventions status, and command and control. These issues can be minimized or even overcome, however, if this integrated relationship is managed in a coordinated manner that best preserves the combatant commander's flexibility in battle by capitalizing on the strengths and capabilities that each agency brings to the fight.

ADDITIONAL ISSUES ASSOCIATED WITH INTEGRATED CIA-SOF WARFIGHTING.

Three additional concerns associated with integrated CIA-SOF warfighting merit comment.

CAPABILITIES-SHIFTING

We must be careful to capitalize on what the CIA brings to the fight, not give them a military mission to execute in DOD's stead. While the CIA's covert paramilitary capability is a valuable and attractive means of operation compared to the usual "noise" of military combat operations, both agencies must be careful to ensure that their integrated operations do not negatively affect the positive capabilities of each. For example, is CIA-SOF warfighting integration true capabilities-shifting, *i.e.*, a reasonable means of "outsourcing" by the National Security Council in order to use the CIA as supplemental warfighters alongside SOF? Or, is such integration merely burden-shifting from the DOD to the CIA based on the CIA's high-speed low-drag flexibility and reduced span of complexity? If it is burden-shifting by the DOD, how would this affect DOD writ large as the various military departments transform themselves to deal more effectively and efficiently with future threats? These policy implications suggest strongly that we must capitalize on each agency's strength and capabilities in combat, not cannibalize each other's missions or shift unwanted burdens.

CONGRESSIONAL OVERSIGHT

It is difficult for Congress to provide effective oversight of integrated CIA and SOF operations, as different sets of committees with disparate agendas and jurisdictions attend this issue. The ways by which the U.S. Congress funds and oversees both the CIA and DOD may not be optimized to support their evolving and overlapping mission in the war against terrorism.[136] Further, it is already difficult to provide effective and seamless oversight of intelligence activities and military operations abroad;[137] to attempt to do so over shared missions imposes an even greater challenge. For covert operations to remain a legitimate national tool, however, this very accountability and control are vital. The fact that Congressional oversight will be more difficult does not militate against the viability of integrated CIA-SOF combat operations as a legitimate tool of U.S. foreign policy.

TARGETING

Both SOF and CIA personnel on the ground in Afghanistan have provided "real-time and near-real-time" targeting data – using either laser designators or radios and laptops to call in global positioning system coordinates to U.S. aircraft flying over the battlefield.[138] Yet there were difficulties in a few of the new targeting tactics, techniques, and procedures (TTPs) that had to be hurriedly fielded between the CIA and DOD, and even though the targeting tactics, techniques, and procedures were improved on the battlefield as the war progressed, "as many as a dozen opportunities to strike high-value but time-critical targets" were lost in the first weeks of the war in Afghanistan.[139] Some of these problems were due to interoperability issues between the CIA and DOD, while others were due to "the length of the decision loop – the time required from when a sensor detects a target to when it can be identified and approved by a human operator."[140] Nevertheless, when compared to each other, the CIA's targeting process is usually quicker, more fluid, and encompasses fewer decision-makers in its "trigger-pulling chain of command" than DOD's[141] According to one anonymous senior defense official in November 2002, today's military is still not designed to move with speed or agility, despite its success in Afghanistan.[142]

Target engagement in integrated CIA-SOF operations involves another major coordination concern, namely, the increased difficulties in preventing friendly fire incidents on battlefields where other government agencies are operating, like Afghanistan. For example, during Operation Anaconda in Afghanistan in March 2002, CIA assets operating on the ground wanted large No Fire Areas over each of their positions, "many of which covered key terrain of interest" to the joint and coalition unconventional warfare and special reconnaissance teams.[143] The use of large No Fire Areas would have denied these unconventional warfare and special reconnaissance teams the flexibility they needed to engage targets in those areas. To address this problem, Coalition Joint Task Force - Mountain (CJTF-Mountain) employed Restricted Fire Areas instead. Restricted Fire Areas enabled the approving ground tactical commander to engage targets he deemed necessary, while facilitating unconventional warfare and special reconnaissance team movement and allowing the commander to set the conditions for future engagements,[144] and continuing to provide friendly fire protection for all concerned. Keeping up to date with all of the CIA assets and non-government agency personnel on the ground and their changing locations was often a significant challenge, however. Although CJTF-Mountain executed an incredibly effective and successful targeting plan while meeting the legitimate concerns of the CIA and non-government agencies, this issue is critical. To prevent fratricide on a battlefield such as that confronted in Afghanistan, where there is no clear front or rear, all participants must work together before the fight to establish interoperable communications in targeting cells and intelligence fusion centers, as well as same-meaning terminology - with all forces clear on the operational terminology and the meaning of those terms.[145]

RECOMMENDATION

In order to win the war on terrorism decisively and with dispatch, the President should continue this new policy of employing CIA paramilitary operatives in a warfighting role alongside SOF in combat. To better manage this new policy, however, the CIA and DOD should jointly develop clear, well-understood procedures that ensure close and effective coordination and that provide for the seamless sharing of battlefield information.

Interagency coordination and cohesion of strategy are the vital links in this new template for warfare.[146] To implement this new policy and ensure a seamless sharing of battlefield information and a consolidated unity of effort on the battlefield, the Joint Interagency Coordinating Group at each combatant command should develop or expand as appropriate the following:

Joint Interagency Coordinating Groups. These groups, headquartered at each unified combatant command, should be composed of liaison officers from any and all organizations that can potentially be helpful to the combatant commander.

Interagency Coordination Annex (Annex V).[147] An Annex V should be included in every combatant command contingency plan to ensure the integration of all pertinent instruments of national power into the combatant commander's deliberate planning process, and to articulate the combatant commander's criteria for entry and exit conditions for other U.S. Government agencies during an operation. Annex V should also serve as the combatant commander's vehicle to identify major missions and tasks for interagency coordination; to identify interagency issues arising with each phase of military operations; to develop follow-on interagency political-military planning; and to request other relevant interagency activities.[148]

New Procedures to Govern Integrated Operations. These procedures should address doctrine, training, policies, and coordination, to ensure their synchronization on the battlefield. Herein lies a thorny thicket of command and control issues, which should be resolved in a manner that provides the combatant commander with more sharply focused unity of command, and the requisite authority -- however defined and accomplished -- over CIA operatives during combat operations to accomplish his assigned tasks. Unity of command necessarily requires clearly defined authorities, roles, and relationships.[149] If CIA operatives are going to be involved in warfighting missions on the battlefield, then they should be responsible to the combatant commander in some organized and formal shape or form.

Laws of War. A working group should be established to formally develop procedures to protect SOF forces from inadvertently violating the Laws of War when they intermingle their operations with CIA operations. This working group should also study and develop legal bases to protect CIA paramilitary operatives and associated SOF from allegations that they are unlawful combatants (this is an issue only for periods of legally recognized armed conflict).

Training Plan. An interagency training plan should be developed to delineate and incorporate coordination measures.

Training Exercise. An interagency training exercise should take place to validate the training plan and coordination measures.

Memorandum of Understanding. This memorandum of understanding should be between the CIA and DOD (and any other agency as deemed necessary) and should outline the authorities and responsibilities of both agencies when they operate together in combat in order to ensure unity of effort.

Although there is no overarching interagency doctrine that specifies or even dictates the procedures and relationships governing all organizations involved in interagency operations, Joint Publication 3-08, Interagency Coordination During Joint Operations, and Presidential Decision Directive-56, Managing Complex Contingency Operations, provide useful general guidance and procedures for planning and managing complex operations.[150]

CONCLUSION

Changed international realities require the U.S. to adapt its response to transnational threats by employing CIA paramilitary operatives in a warfighting role alongside SOF. According to former Senate Intelligence Committee Chairman Bob Graham, Democrat - Florida, "The type of combat we're likely to be in from now on is not World War II, with mass tank attacks, but rather this type of small-unit operation where good intelligence, operational intelligence is the key to your success. . . . We've asked the question [about coordination] consistently . . . and we've gotten . . . increasingly positive statements about the close and effective relationship between intelligence and war fighters."[151] This integration blurs organizational boundaries, however, and for policy reasons, legal protections, and operational effectiveness, we must develop new procedures to deal with these blurred boundaries. Further, there is a concomitant need for both groups to maintain a well-delineated separation between themselves. Without this separation, we risk losing the political and military value of covert operations, and invite the perception that we are attempting to avoid customary international law and the laws of war by disguising SOF operations as CIA operations or, more likely, vice versa.

Because America's political-military activities are increasingly colored by self-imposed legal constraints as well as the weight of world opinion, choosing between CIA covert action, military action, or a combination of the two, presents important and difficult challenges to America's senior policy-makers. Competing interests must be weighed and balanced, and compromises will surely have to be made.[152] In that the political object to be had by war will affect not only the level of effort to be made but also the conduct of the operations, it is also appropriate to quote Carl von Clausewitz, who rejected the idea that there is only one "best path to victory, finding instead that 'many roads lead to success.'"[153]

Word Count = 10,740

25

ENDNOTES

[1] In October 1996, Uzbek and Tajik factions in the geographical northern third of Afghanistan formed the "Northern Alliance" to combat the Taliban. Since then the Northern Alliance became known as the umbrella grouping of anti-Taliban forces in Afghanistan. *See* "Country Profile: Afghanistan," World News Digest, 29 August 2002; available from http://www.2facts.com/ancillaries/index/c00002.asp.html; Internet; accessed 29 August 2002. *See also* "Afghanistan - Countrywatch;" available from http://www.countrywatch.com/cw_topic.asp?vCOUNTRY=1&SECTION=SUB&TOPIC=POPCO&T.html; Internet; accessed 29 August 2002.

[2] Osama bin Laden is an Islamic fundamentalist believed by intelligence officials to be the leader of Al Qaeda, an international terrorist network. *See* Endnote 6, *supra*. Bin Laden was born in Saudi Arabia in 1957 to a Yemeni-born Saudi billionaire. Osama bin Laden left Saudi Arabia in 1991 after aiding groups opposed to the reigning Fahd family, taking his $250 million inheritance with him. Bin Laden's sworn hostility to the United States purportedly stems from Saudi Arabia's 1990 decision to permit the U.S. to station troops on Saudi soil after Iraq invaded Kuwait. Bin Laden has issued *fatwahs* (religious rulings) encouraging Muslims to kill Americans. *See* "Facts on Osama bin Laden," World News Digest, 29 August 2002; available from http://www.2facts.com/ancillaries/index/b00222.asp.html; Internet; accessed 29 August 2002.

[3] Al Qaeda (Arabic for "the base") is an international terrorist network formed around 1987 by Osama bin Laden and militants from the Egyptian Islamic Jihad as a base for their worldwide crusade. *See* "Facts on Osama bin Laden," World News Digest, 29 August 2002; available from http://www.2facts.com/ancillaries/index/b00222.asp.html; Internet; accessed 29 August 2002. Al Qaeda "terrorists practice a fringe form of Islamic extremism that has been rejected by Muslim scholars and the vast majority of Muslim clerics . . . The terrorists' directive commands them to kill Christians and Jews, to kill all Americans and make no distinctions among military and civilians, including women and children." *See* "World Trade Center and Pentagon Terrorist Attacks: Transcript of Bush's Speech to Congress," World News Digest, 27 September 2002; available from http://www.2facts.com/stories/index/2001227310.asp.html; Internet; accessed 29 August 2002.

[4] Bob Woodward, Bush at War (New York: Simon & Schuster, 2002), 40. *See also* Bob Drogin, "U.S. Had Plan for Covert Afghan Options Before 9/11," Los Angeles Times, sec. A, p. 14 (1074 words) [database on-line]; available from Lexis-Nexis; accessed 29 August 2002.

[5] United Airlines Flight # 93 crashed near Shanksville, Pennsylvania when passengers fought back against four terrorists who had hijacked the airliner. Passengers learned from cellular telephone calls with family members and friends on the ground that three other airliners had been hijacked minutes earlier and flown into the Twin Towers and the Pentagon. Because the terrorists had turned Flight # 93 back east, away from its intended West Coast destination, passengers believed the hijackers were trying to fly the plane back to a target in the D.C. area when they fought back. Several months later, U.S. officials said that captured senior Al Qaeda leader Abu Zubaydah had told them that Flight 93 was intended to hit the White House on 11 September 2001. *See* "White House Target of Flight 93, Officials Say," CNN.COM, 23 May 2002; available from http://www.cnn.com/2002/US/05/23/flight.93/index.html; Internet; accessed 17 March 2003.

[6] An "act of terrorism" means an activity that involves a violent act or an act dangerous to human life that is a violation of the criminal laws of the United States or of any State . . . and appears to be intended to intimidate or coerce a civilian population; to influence the policy of a government by intimidation or coercion; or to affect the conduct of a government by assassination or kidnapping. Title 18, U.S. Code, Section 3077, Definitions (Section 3077 is a part of Chapter 204, Rewards for Information Concerning Terrorist Acts and Espionage). DOD Directive 2000.12, DOD Antiterrorism/Force Protection (ATFP) Program, 13 April 1999, defines "terrorism" as the "calculated use of violence or threat of violence to inculcate fear; intended to coerce or to intimidate governments or societies in the pursuit of goals that are generally political, religious, or ideological." Department of Defense, DOD Antiterrorism/Force Protection (ATFP) Program, Department of Defense Directive 2000.12 (Washington, D.C.: U.S. Department of Defense, 1 April 1999).

[7] Amy Westfeldt, "9/11 Cost for NYC Tops $33 Billion," The Patriot-News, 13 November 2002, sec. A, p. 8. The total worldwide economic loss impact has been estimated to top $600 billion, a "strategically significant" event according to remarks made by a speaker participating in the Commandant's Lecture Series at the Army War College in 2002.

[8] "The deliberate and deadly attacks, which were carried out yesterday against our country, were more than acts of terror. They were acts of war." See "Hijacked Jets Destroy World Trade Center, Hit Pentagon: Text of President Bush's September 12 Statement," World News Digest, 13 September 2001; available from http://www.2facts.com/stories/index/2001226370.asp.html; Internet; accessed 29 August 2002. See also United States Congress, Report on Actions Taken to Respond to the Threat of Terrorism Communication from the President of the United States Transmitting a Report, Consistent with the War Powers Resolution and Senate Joint Resolution 23, to Help Ensure that the Congress is Kept Fully Informed on Actions Taken to Respond to the Threat of Terrorism, 107th Cong., 1st sess., 25 September 2001. This report became House Document 107-127. See also United States Congress, Senate Joint Resolution 23: Authorization for Use of United States Armed Forces, 107th Cong., 1st sess., 14 September 2001. This joint resolution became Public Law on September 20, 2001 (see P.L. 107-40).

[9] United States Congress, Senate Joint Resolution 23: Authorization for Use of United States Armed Forces, 107th Cong., 1st sess., 14 September 2002. This joint resolution became Public Law on September 20, 2002 (see P.L. 107-40).

[10] Bob Woodward, "Secret CIA Units Playing a Central Combat Role," The Washington Post, 18 November 2001, sec. A, p. 1 [database on-line]; available from ProQuest; accessed 29 August 2002. See also Presidential Approval and Reporting of Covert Actions, U.S. Code, Title 50, sec. 413b (2002).

[11] Jim Pavitt, Deputy Director for Operations, Central Intelligence Agency, Text of Address to Duke University Law School Conference (as delivered), 11 April 2002; available from http://www.cia.gov/cia/public_affairs/speeches/archives/2002/pavitt_04262002.html; Internet; accessed 17 March 2003. See also Maxim Kniazkov, "CIA Creates Super Secret Hit Team to Target Terrorists Abroad," Agence France Presse, 4 June 2002, p. 1 (547 words) [database on-line]; available from Lexis-Nexis; accessed 29 August 2002.

[12] Ibid., 101, 134-135.

[13] United States Congress, <u>Report on Actions Taken to Respond to the Threat of Terrorism Communication from the President of the United States Transmitting a Report, Consistent with the War Powers Resolution and Senate Joint Resolution 23, to Help Ensure that the Congress is Kept Fully Informed on Actions Taken to Respond to the Threat of Terrorism</u>, 107th Cong., 1st sess., 25 September 2001. This report became House Document 107-127. *See also* Alexander Hamilton, "Federalist No. 74: The Command of the Military and Naval Forces, and the Pardoning Power of the Executive," <u>Federalist Papers</u>, from the New York Packet, 25 March 1788 ("The President of the United States is to be commander-in-chief of the army and navy of the United States, and of the militia of the several States when called into the actual service of the United States.").

[14] On September 27, 1996, members of the Islamic Taliban (Religious Students Movement), a Moslem fundamentalist group composed largely of former theology students, displaced the ruling members of the Afghan Government and declared themselves -- the Taliban -- the legitimate government of Afghanistan. The Taliban were never recognized by the United Nations. *See* "CIA -- The World Factbook -- Afghanistan;" available from http://www.cia.gov.cia/publications/factbook/geos/af.html; Internet; accessed 29 August 2002. *See also* "Afghanistan - Countrywatch;" available from http://www.countrywatch.com/cw_topic.asp?vCOUNTRY=1&SECTION=SUB&TOPIC=POPCO&T.html; Internet; accessed 29 August 2002.

[15] "Bush's Address Announcing Military Strikes Against Afghanistan: Text," <u>World News Digest</u>, 11 October 2001; available from http://www.2facts.com/stories/index/2001228130.asp.html; Internet; accessed 29 August 2002.

[16] The CQ Researcher, <u>Intelligence Reforms</u>, Washington, D.C.: CQ Press, 25 January 2002, vol. 12, no. 3. *See also* Bob Woodward, <u>Bush at War</u> (New York: Simon & Schuster, 2002), 139.

[17] See Endnote 1, *supra*.

[18] Bob Woodward, <u>Bush at War</u> (New York: Simon & Schuster, 2002), 101, 134, 141. *See also* Associated Press, "CIA Plays High-Profile Military Role in Afghanistan with US-CIA-Shadow Army," <u>Associated Press Worldstream</u>, 20 May 2002, p.1 (379 words) [database on-line]; available from Lexis-Nexis; accessed 29 August 2002; *and* Evan Thomas and Colin Soloway, "A Street Fight," <u>Newsweek</u>, 29 April 2002, sec. International, p. 30 (2596 words) [database on-line]; available from Lexis-Nexis; accessed 29 August 2002. *See also* Bob Woodward, <u>Bush at War</u> (New York: Simon & Schuster, 2002), 193.

[19] Bob Woodward, <u>Bush at War</u> (New York: Simon & Schuster, 2002), 101, 134.

[20] "World Trade Center and Pentagon Terrorist Attacks: Transcript of Bush's Speech to Congress," <u>World News Digest</u>, 27 September 2002; available from http://www.2facts.com/stories/index/2001227310.asp.html; Internet; accessed 29 August 2002.

[21] Bob Woodward, <u>Bush at War</u> (New York: Simon & Schuster, 2002), 90.

[22] Richard B. Myers, National Military Strategy of the United States of America (Pre-Decisional Draft) (Washington, D.C.: The Pentagon, 19 September 2002).

[23] *See generally* Pat M. Holt, <u>Secret Intelligence and Public Policy - A Dilemma of Democracy</u> (Washington, D.C.: Congressional Quarterly Inc., 1995), 149-156.

[24] Bob Woodward, "CIA Told to Do 'Whatever Necessary' to Kill Bin Laden," <u>The Washington Post</u>, 21 October 2001; available from <u>http://www.washingtonpost.com/ac2/wp-dyn/A27452-2001Oct20</u>; Internet; accessed 26 September 2002. *See also* Associated Press, "CIA Plays High-Profile Military Role in Afghanistan with US-CIA-Shadow Army," <u>Associated Press Worldstream</u>, 20 May 2002, p.1 (379 words) [database on-line]; available from Lexis-Nexis; accessed 29 August 2002. *See also generally* Ronald Kessler, <u>Inside the CIA - Revealing the Secrets of the World's Most Powerful Spy Agency</u> (New York: Pocket Books, 1992); *and* Charles D. Ameringer, <u>U.S. Foreign Intelligence - The Secret Side of American History</u> (Lexington, Massachusetts: Lexington Books, 1990).

[25] Bob Woodward, "CIA Told to Do 'Whatever Necessary' to Kill Bin Laden," <u>The Washington Post</u>, 21 October 2001; available from <u>http://www.washingtonpost.com/ac2/wp-dyn/A27452-2001Oct20</u>; Internet; accessed 26 September 2002. *See also* Bob Woodward, <u>Bush at War</u> (New York: Simon & Schuster, 2002), 166.

[26] Ibid.

[27] Dana Priest, "'Team 555' Shaped a New Way of War; Special Forces and Smart Bombs Turned Tide and Routed Taliban," <u>The Washington Post - Final Edition</u>, 3 April 2002, sec. A, p. 1 (4014 words) [database on-line]; available from Lexis-Nexis; accessed 29 August 2002.

[28] Ibid. "Phil [from the CIA's analytical branch] gave a briefing on the mission: The next day, the team [SOF Team 555] would join up with commanders allied with Massoud's successor, Gen. Mohammed Fahim, the Northern Alliance's defense minister. . . . First, they [Team 555] were to help U.S. warplanes destroy the Taliban front line around that airfield. Then, they were to search for and destroy Taliban and Al Qaeda targets in the 35-mile stretch south to Kabul. Finally, they were to help the alliance seize Kabul . . . When Phil introduced [the team members] to Bismullah Khan at their next safe house . . . he said, 'Here's the Special Forces team I've been promising you.'" *See also* Jonathan Weisman, "CIA, Pentagon Feuding Complicates War Effort," <u>USA Today</u>, 17 June 2002, sec. A, p. 11 (1534 words) [database on-line]; available from Lexis-Nexis; accessed 29 August 2002.

[29] Bryan Bender, Kim Burger, and Andrew Koch, "Afghanistan: First Lessons," <u>Jane's Special Reports</u>, 14 December 2001; available from <u>http://www.janes.com.html</u>; Internet; accessed 12 September 2002.

[30] Bob Woodward, <u>Bush at War</u> (New York: Simon & Schuster, 2002), 166.

[31] Ibid., 202.

[32] Thom Shanker and James Risen, "Rumsfeld Weighs New Covert Acts by Military Units," <u>The New York Times, Late Edition - Final</u>, 12 August 2002, sec. A, p. 1 (1604 words) [database on-line]; available from Lexis-Nexis; accessed 29 August 2002.

[33] Ibid.

[34] *See* Endnote 19, *supra*.

[35] Jim Pavitt, Deputy Director for Operations, Central Intelligence Agency, Text of Address to Duke University Law School Conference (as delivered), 11 April 2002; available from http://www.cia.gov/cia/public_affairs/speeches/archives/2002/pavitt_04262002.html; Internet; accessed 17 March 2003. *See also* Bob Drogin, "U.S. Had Plan for Covert Afghan Options Before 9/11," Los Angeles Times, sec. A, p. 14 (1074 words) [database on-line]; available from Lexis-Nexis; accessed 29 August 2002.

[36] J. Daniel Moore, "CIA Support to Operation Enduring Freedom," Military Intelligence Professional Bulletin, vol. 28, iss. 3 (Jul-Sep 2002): 46 [database on-line]; available from ProQuest; accessed 29 August 2002.

[37] Ron Kampeas, "CIA's Paramilitary Scores Successes," Associated Press Online, 20 May 2002, p. 1 (968 words) [database on-line]; available from Lexis-Nexis; accessed 29 August 2002. *See also* Bryan Bender, Kim Burger, and Andrew Koch, "Afghanistan: First Lessons," Jane's Special Reports, 14 December 2001; available from http://www.janes.com.html; Internet; accessed 12 September 2002 ("U.S. Defense Secretary Donald Rumsfeld has denied any coordination problems, saying the CIA forces on the ground 'are tucked in very tight with the U.S. military.'")

[38] *See* Constitution of the United States, Article I, Section 8; and Article II, Section 2.

[39] *See generally* Armed Forces, U.S. Code, Title 10 (2002).

[40] Department of Defense, Functions of the Department of Defense and Its Major Components, Department of Defense Directive 5100.1 (Washington, D.C.: U.S. Department of Defense, 1 August 2002), 4.

[41] The mission to capture Arnold was aborted when Arnold's change in travel plans made his capture impossible. *See* "Intelligence Operations (Wartime Special Operations)," 2 October 2002; available from http://www.cia.gov/csi/books/warindep/intellopos.html; Internet; accessed 2 October 2002. Other examples of special operations in the colonial era include Major Robert Rogers, who led the New England Companies of Rangers in the French and Indian War; Francis Marion (aka the "Swamp Fox"), a guerilla leader during the American Revolutionary War; and Sergeant Ezra Lee, who used an oak submersible to attack a British frigate in New York Harbor in August 1776. *See* United States Special Operations Command, Special Operations in Peace and War, United States Special Operations Command Pub 1 (Washington, D.C.: U.S. Special Operations Command, 25 January 1996), 2-2.

[42] Goldwater-Nichols Department of Defense Reorganization Act of 1986, Public Law 99-433, 99th U.S. Congress, October 1, 1986, codified at U.S. Code, Title 10, Subtitle A, Part 1, Chapter 5. With respect to Special Operations Forces in particular, *see* Unified Combatant Command for Special Operations Forces, U.S. Code, Title 50, section 167 (2002).

[43] Rowan Scarborough, "Rumsfeld Gives 'Blank Sheet' to Update Special Operations," The Washington Times, 21 November 2002, p. 15.

[44] For a list of special operations activities, *see* Unified Combatant Command for Special Operations Forces, U.S. Code, Title 10, sec. 167(j) (2002). *See also* United States Special Operations Command, Special Operations in Peace and War, United States Special Operations

Command Pub 1 (Washington, D.C.: U.S. Special Operations Command, 25 January 1996), 3-2 – 3-6.

[45] United States Special Operations Command, Special Operations in Peace and War, United States Special Operations Command Pub 1 (Washington, D.C.: U.S. Special Operations Command, 25 January 1996), 3-1.

[46] Ibid, 1-1.

[47] The term "unified combatant command" means a military command which has broad, continuing missions and which is composed of forces from two or more military departments." Combatant Commands: Establishment, U.S. Code, Title 10, sec. 161(c)(1) (2002).

[48] Unified Combatant Command for Special Operations Forces, U.S. Code, Title 10, sec. 167(d) (2002).

[49] John M. Shalikashvili, National Military Strategy of the United States of America (Washington, D.C.: The Pentagon, September 1997), 5.

[50] Richard B. Myers, National Military Strategy of the United States of America (Pre-Decisional Draft) (Washington, D.C.: The Pentagon, 19 September 2002), 14.

[51] National Security Act of 1947, Public Law 235, 61 Stat. 496, July 26, 1947, codified in various portions of Titles 10, 32, and 50 of the U.S. Code.

[52] Ibid.

[53] Harry Rositzke, The CIA's Secret Operations (New York: Reader's Digest Press, 1977), xviii. See also John Jay, "Federalist No. 64: The Powers of the Senate," Federalist Papers, from the New York Packet, 7 March 1788; and Article II, Section 2, Constitution of the United States, which provides the President with the power to make treaties, with the advice and consent of the Senate.

[54] All duties and responsibilities of the CIA shall be related to the intelligence functions set out in paragraph 1.8 of Executive Order 12333; and as authorized by the National Security Act of 1947, as amended; the CIA Act of 1949, as amended; and other appropriate directives or other applicable law. See Executive Order 12333--United States Intelligence Activities, paragraph 1.8, 46 Federal Register 59941, 3 CFR, 1981 Comp., p. 200; also available from http://www.cia.gov/cia/information/eo12333.html; Internet; accessed 29 September 2002. See also George J. Tenet, The Authorities and Responsibilities of the Director of Central Intelligence as Head of the U.S. Intelligence Community, Director of Central Intelligence Directive 1/1 (Washington, D.C.: Director of Central Intelligence, 19 November 1998), para's 7.a, 7.c.

[55] Ibid.

[56] Executive Order 12333--United States Intelligence Activities, paragraph 3.4(h), 46 Federal Register 59941, 3 CFR, 1981 Comp., p. 200; also available from http://www.cia.gov/cia/information/eo12333.html; Internet; accessed 29 September 2002.

[57] Ibid.

[58] Pat M. Holt, <u>Secret Intelligence and Public Policy - A Dilemma of Democracy</u> (Washington, D.C.: Congressional Quarterly Inc., 1995), 136.

[59] <u>Intelligence Authorization Act, Fiscal Year 1991</u>, <u>Statutes at Large</u> 105, sec. 602, 443 (1991) [Public Law 102-88, 14 August 1991]; *See also* <u>War and National Defense, National Security: Presidential Approval and Reporting of Covert Actions</u>, U.S. Code, Title 50, section 413b(e) (2002); *and* Pat M. Holt, <u>Secret Intelligence and Public Policy - A Dilemma of Democracy</u>, (Washington, D.C.: Congressional Quarterly Inc., 1995), 136.

[60] <u>War and National Defense, National Security: Presidential Approval and Reporting of Covert Actions</u>, U.S. Code, Title 50, section 413b(e) (2002).

[61] Charles D. Ameringer, <u>U.S. Foreign Intelligence - The Secret Side of American History</u> (Lexington, Massachusetts: Lexington Books, 1990), 392.

[62] Stansfield Turner, "Intelligence and Secrecy in an Open Society," <u>The Center Magazine</u> XIX, no. 2 (March/April 1986): 4.

[63] Ibid.

[64] John M. Oseth, <u>Regulating U.S. Intelligence Operations</u> (Lexington: The University Press of Kentucky, 1985), 36. *See also generally* National Security Act of 1947. Get cite.

[65] Ronald Kessler, <u>Inside the CIA - Revealing the Secrets of the World's Most Powerful Spy Agency</u> (New York: Pocket Books, 1992), 237.

[66] John M. Oseth, <u>Regulating U.S. Intelligence Operations</u> (Lexington: The University Press of Kentucky, 1985), 136. *See also* Sec. 102(d)(5) (50 U.S.C. 403-3) of the National Security Act of 1947, as amended, at Public Law 235, 61 Stat. 496, July 26, 1947.

[67] John M. Oseth, <u>Regulating U.S. Intelligence Operations</u> (Lexington: The University Press of Kentucky, 1985), 136.

[68] Ibid, 36.

[69] Harry Rositzke, <u>The CIA's Secret Operations</u> (New York: Reader's Digest Press, 1977), 155.

[70] Ronald Kessler, <u>Inside the CIA - Revealing the Secrets of the World's Most Powerful Spy Agency</u> (New York: Pocket Books, 1992), 237-238.

[71] Ibid, 238.

[72] Ibid.

[73] Harry Rositzke, <u>The CIA's Secret Operations</u> (New York: Reader's Digest Press, 1977), xvi.

[74] Ibid, 152.

⁷⁵ War and National Defense, National Security: Presidential Approval and Reporting of Covert Actions, U.S. Code, Title 50, section 413b(a) and (a)(1) (2002). *See also* Intelligence Authorization Act, Fiscal Year 1991, Public Law 102-88 [H.R. 1455]; 14 August 1991; title VI, sec. 503. *See also* footnote 9, *supra*.

⁷⁶ War and National Defense, National Security: Presidential Approval and Reporting of Covert Actions, U.S. Code, Title 50, section 413b(a)(3) (2002).

⁷⁷ Ibid, 413b(a)(5). *See also* Pat M. Holt, Secret Intelligence and Public Policy - A Dilemma of Democracy (Washington, D.C.: Congressional Quarterly Inc., 1995), 158.

⁷⁸ "Intelligence Operations (Covert Action)," 2 October 2002; available from http://www.cia.gov/csi/books/warindep/intellopos.html; Internet; accessed 2 October 2002.

⁷⁹ J. Daniel Moore, "CIA Support to Operation Enduring Freedom," Military Intelligence Professional Bulletin, vol. 28, iss. 3 (Jul-Sep 2002): 46 [database on-line]; available from ProQuest; accessed 29 August 2002.

⁸⁰ Ibid. *See also* Charles D. Ameringer, U.S. Foreign Intelligence - The Secret Side of American History (Lexington, Massachusetts: Lexington Books, 1990), 168.

⁸¹ Charles D. Ameringer, U.S. Foreign Intelligence - The Secret Side of American History (Lexington, Massachusetts: Lexington Books, 1990), 168.

⁸² Ibid.

⁸³ Ibid.

⁸⁴ Central Intelligence Agency, Center for the Study of Intelligence, Central Intelligence: Origin and Evolution (Washington, D.C.: U.S. Government Printing Office, September 2001), 13.

⁸⁵ Ibid.

⁸⁶ Ibid.

⁸⁷ Ibid, 14.

⁸⁸ Bob Woodward, "CIA Told to Do 'Whatever Necessary' to Kill Bin Laden," The Washington Post, 21 October 2001; available from http://www.washingtonpost.com/ac2/wp-dyn/A27452-2001Oct20; Internet; accessed 26 September 2002. *See also* Evan Thomas and Colin Soloway, "A Street Fight," Newsweek, 29 April 2002, sec. International, p. 30 (2596 words) [database on-line]; available from Lexis-Nexis; accessed 29 August 2002; *and* Bob Woodward, "Secret CIA Units Playing a Central Combat Role," The Washington Post, 18 November 2001, sec. A, p. 1 [database on-line]; available from ProQuest; accessed 29 August 2002.

⁸⁹ Alan E. Goodman, "Reforming U.S. Intelligence," Foreign Policy, no. 67 (Summer 1987): 131, 133. *See also* John C. Green, Secret Intelligence and Covert Action: Consensus in an Open Society, Strategy Research Project (Carlisle Barracks: U.S. Army War College, 19 March 1993), 29.

[90] Harry Rositzke, "America's Secret Operations: A Perspective," <u>Foreign Affairs</u> 53, no. 2 (January 1975): 344-345, 348. *See also* John C. Green, <u>Secret Intelligence and Covert Action: Consensus in an Open Society</u>, Strategy Research Project (Carlisle Barracks: U.S. Army War College, 19 March 1993), 29.

[91] Congressional Research Service Report for Congress, <u>Intelligence and Law Enforcement: Countering Transnational Threats to the U.S.</u> (Washington, D.C.: The Library of Congress, January 16, 2001), p. CRS-26.

[92] The ideas for this sentence came from William M. Arkin, "Warfare; Dressed -- and Equipped -- to Kill," <u>Los Angeles Times</u>, 4 August 2002, p. M1 [database on-line]; available from ProQuest; accessed 29 August 2002.

[93] Harry Rositzke, <u>The CIA's Secret Operations</u> (New York: Reader's Digest Press, 1977), 166.

[94] Pat M. Holt, <u>Secret Intelligence and Public Policy - A Dilemma of Democracy</u> (Washington, D.C.: Congressional Quarterly Inc., 1995), 159.

[95] Ibid. This begs an obvious political question: What happens if the operation fails, or is compromised? It depends on the nature of the operation, of course. For example, the U.S. might find itself in the position where it must abandon its operatives rather than admit U.S. complicity. Or, the President might face a crisis, such as the failed Desert One mission in April of 1980, that contributes in part to the loss of his office in the next election. This question, although meaningful, addresses an issue that is beyond the scope of this paper.

[96] Congressional Research Service Report for Congress, <u>Intelligence and Law Enforcement: Countering Transnational Threats to the U.S.</u> (Washington, D.C.: The Library of Congress, January 16, 2001), p. CRS-26 – 27. *See also generally* The White House, National Security Strategy of the United States of America 10-12 (2002); available at http://www.whitehouse.gov/nsc/nssall.html.

[97] By their very nature and purpose, CIA covert operations reflect an inability -- or perhaps an unwillingness -- to accept the constraints of acting openly within legal norms and, *ipso facto*, challenge the traditional U.S. values of openness and respect for the sovereignty of other nations. *See* "Special Ops; Exploring New Uses is Appropriate," <u>Star Tribune (Minneapolis, MN)</u>, 19 August 2002, sec. A, p. 10 (432 words) [database on-line]; available from Lexis-Nexis; accessed 29 August 2002. *See also* Congressional Research Service Report for Congress, <u>Intelligence and Law Enforcement: Countering Transnational Threats to the U.S.</u> (Washington, D.C.: The Library of Congress, January 16, 2001), p. CRS-27.

[98] Congressional Research Service Report for Congress, <u>Intelligence and Law Enforcement: Countering Transnational Threats to the U.S.</u> (Washington, D.C.: The Library of Congress, January 16, 2001), p. CRS-26. However, the secrecy of such covert actions, as necessary as they are, and as well understood as that necessity is by other law-abiding nations, does deprive the U.S. of demonstrable evidence that all of our actions in protecting our vital interests are consistent with either national or international law

[99] <u>War and National Defense, National Security: Presidential Approval and Reporting of Covert Actions</u>, U.S. Code, Title 50, section 413b(a) and (a)(1) (2002).

[100] Ronald Kessler, Inside the CIA - Revealing the Secrets of the World's Most Powerful Spy Agency (New York: Pocket Books, 1992), 3.

[101] Quoted in Benjamin Wittes, "Blurring the Line Between Cops and Spies," Legal Times, 9 September 1996, p.20. *See also* Congressional Research Service Report for Congress, Intelligence and Law Enforcement: Countering Transnational Threats to the U.S. (Washington, D.C.: The Library of Congress, January 16, 2001), p. CRS-9; *and* Unified Combatant Command for Special Operations Forces, U.S. Code, Title 10, sec. 167 (2002); *and* Department of Defense, Functions of the Department of Defense and its Major Components, Department of Defense Directive 5100.1 (Washington, D.C.: U.S. Department of Defense, 1 August 2002) 4, 10-11.

[102] Ronald Kessler, Inside the CIA - Revealing the Secrets of the World's Most Powerful Spy Agency (New York: Pocket Books, 1992), 188.

[103] Department of Defense, Law of War Program, Department of Defense Directive 5100.77 (Washington, D.C.: U.S. Department of Defense, 9 December 1998), para. 5.3.1.

[104] *See* Convention for the Amelioration of the Condition of Wounded and Sick in Armed Conflict in the Field, 12 August 1949, art. 2, 6 U.S.T. 3114, 3118, 75 U.N.T.S. 31, 33; Convention for the Amelioration of the Condition of Wounded, Sick and Shipwrecked Members of Armed Forces at Sea, 12 August 1949, art. 2, 6 U.S.T. 3217, 3220, 75 U.N.T.S. 85, 88; Convention Relative to the Treatment of Prisoners of War, 12 August 1949, art. 2, 6 U.S.T. 3316, 3318, 75 U.N.T.S. 135, 137 [Geneva Convention III]; Convention Relative to the Protection of Civilian Persons in Time of War, 12 August 1949, art. 2, 6 U.S.T. 3516, 3518, 75 U.N.T.S. 287, 289 [Geneva Convention IV].

[105] Brigadier General Charles J. Dunlap, Jr., USAF, "International Law and Terrorism: Some 'Qs and As' for Operators," The Army Lawyer, Department of the Army Pamphlet 27-50-357 (October/November 2002): 24.

[106] Charles D. Ameringer, U.S. Foreign Intelligence - The Secret Side of American History (Lexington, Massachusetts: Lexington Books, 1990), 392.

[107] John C. Green, Secret Intelligence and Covert Action: Consensus in an Open Society, Strategy Research Project (Carlisle Barracks: U.S. Army War College, 19 March 1993), 14. *See also* Robert M. Gates, "CIA and Openness," Vital Speeches of the Day LVIII, no. 14 (1 May 1992): 430-431.

[108] War and National Defense, National Security: Presidential Approval and Reporting of Covert Actions, U.S. Code, Title 50, section 413b(a)(5) (2002).

[109] Ron Kampeas, "CIA's Paramilitary Scores Successes," Associated Press Online, 20 May 2002, p. 1 (968 words) [database on-line]; available from Lexis-Nexis; accessed 29 August 2002. *See also* War and National Defense, National Security: Presidential Approval and Reporting of Covert Actions, U.S. Code, Title 50, section 413b(a)(5) (2002).

[110] War and National Defense, National Security, Accountability for Intelligence Activities, General Congressional Oversight Provisions, U.S. Code, Title 50, sec. 413(a) (2002). *See also*

Ron Kampeas, "CIA's Paramilitary Scores Successes," <u>Associated Press Online</u>, 20 May 2002, p. 1 (968 words) [database on-line]; available from Lexis-Nexis; accessed 29 August 2002.

[111] Frank J. Williams, Chief Justice, Supreme Court of Rhode Island, "Letter to the Editor: Abraham Lincoln and Al Qaeda," <u>American Heritage</u>, October 2002, 10-11.

[112] Ibid

[113] *See supra* note 105.

[114] Brigadier General Charles J. Dunlap, Jr., USAF, "International Law and Terrorism: Some 'Qs and As' for Operators," <u>The Army Lawyer</u>, Department of the Army Pamphlet 27-50-357 (October/November 2002): 24-25, 29. *See also generally supra* note 105.

[115] Goldwater-Nichols Department of Defense Reorganization Act of 1986, Public Law 99-433, 99th U.S. Congress, October 1, 1986, codified at U.S. Code, Title 10, Subtitle A, Part 1, Chapter 5.

[116] <u>Commanders of Combatant Commands: Assignment; Powers and Duties</u>, U.S. Code, Title 10, sec. 164 (2002).

[117] Susan Schmidt and Thomas E. Ricks, "Pentagon Plans Shift in War on Terror: Special Operations Command's Role to Grow with Covert Approach," <u>The Washington Post</u>, 18 September 2002, p. 1 [database on-line]; available from https://www.us.army.mil/portal/jhtml/earlyBird/Sep2002/e20020918pentagon.htm; accessed 18 September 2002.

[118] <u>Combatant Commands: Assigned Forces; Chain of Command</u>, U.S. Code, Title 10, sec. 162 (2002).

[119] <u>Commanders of Combatant Commands: Assignment; Powers and Duties</u>, U.S. Code, Title 10, sec. 164(b)(1) (2002). The Goldwater-Nichols Department of Defense Reorganization Act of 1986 makes the following statement of policy: "In enacting this Act, it is the intent of Congress, consistent with the congressional declaration of policy in section 2 of the National Security Act of 1947 (50 U.S.C. 401) - . . . (3) to place clear responsibility on the commanders of the unified and specified combatant commands for the accomplishment of missions assigned to those commands." *See* Joint Chiefs of Staff, <u>Unified Action Armed Forces (UNAAF)</u>, Joint Publication 0-2 (Washington, D.C.: Joint Chiefs of Staff, 10 July 2001), I-2.

[120] Department of Defense, <u>Functions of the Department of Defense and Its Major Components</u>, Department of Defense Directive 5100.1 (Washington, D.C.: U.S. Department of Defense, 1 August 2002), 11.

[121] <u>Commanders of Combatant Commands: Assignment; Powers and Duties</u>, U.S. Code, Title 10, sec. 164(d)(1) (2002).

[122] Nathan Hodge, "CIA's Predator Behavior is Cause for Concern," <u>Newsday</u>, 6 June 2002, sec. Viewpoints, p. A49 (979 words) [database on-line]; available from Lexis-Nexis; accessed 29 August 2002.

[123] Ibid. Hodge's viewpoint is consistent with Presidential Decision Directive (PDD) - 35 issued by President Clinton, which instructs the Intelligence Community to provide military commanders with the tactical intelligence they need in operations. *See* Central Intelligence Agency, Center for the Study of Intelligence. <u>Central Intelligence: Origin and Evolution</u> (Washington, D.C.: U.S. Government Printing Office, September 2001), 13.

[124] Nathan Hodge, "CIA's Predator Behavior is Cause for Concern," <u>Newsday</u>, 6 June 2002, sec. Viewpoints, p. A49 (979 words) [database on-line]; available from Lexis-Nexis; accessed 29 August 2002.

[125] Jonathan Weisman, "CIA, Pentagon Feuding Complicates War Effort," <u>USA Today</u>, 17 June 2002, sec. A, p. 11 (1534 words) [database on-line]; available from Lexis-Nexis; accessed 29 August 2002.

[126] Ibid.

[127] Douglas Waller, "Inside the CIA's Covert Forces," <u>Time</u>, 10 December 2001, p. 56 [database on-line]; available from ProQuest; accessed 29 August 2002.

[128] Bob Woodward, <u>Bush at War</u> (New York: Simon & Schuster, 2002), 193-194.

[129] Bob Woodward, "Secret CIA Units Playing a Central Combat Role," <u>The Washington Post</u>, 18 November 2001, sec. A, p. 1 [database on-line]; available from ProQuest; accessed 29 August 2002.

[130] The idea, and number figures, for this sentence and its point of view came from Thom Shanker and James Risen, "Rumsfeld Weighs New Covert Acts by Military Units," <u>The New York Times, Late Edition - Final</u>, 12 August 2002, sec. A, p. 1 (1604 words) [database on-line]; available from Lexis-Nexis; accessed 29 August 2002.

[131] Ron Kampeas, "CIA's Paramilitary Scores Successes," <u>Associated Press Online</u>, 20 May 2002, p. 1 (968 words) [database on-line]; available from Lexis-Nexis; accessed 29 August 2002. *See also* Thom Shanker and James Risen, "Rumsfeld Weighs New Covert Acts by Military Units," <u>The New York Times, Late Edition - Final</u>, 12 August 2002, sec. A, p. 1 (1604 words) [database on-line]; available from Lexis-Nexis; accessed 29 August 2002.

[132] The CQ Researcher, <u>Intelligence Reforms,</u> Washington, D.C.: CQ Press, 25 January 2002, vol. 12, no. 3.

[133] Ron Kampeas, "CIA's Paramilitary Scores Successes," <u>Associated Press Online</u>, 20 May 2002, p. 1 (968 words) [database on-line]; available from Lexis-Nexis; accessed 29 August 2002.

[134] Congressional Research Service Report for Congress, <u>Intelligence and Law Enforcement: Countering Transnational Threats to the U.S.</u> (Washington, D.C.: The Library of Congress, January 16, 2001), p. CRS-14.

[135] Evan Thomas and Colin Soloway, "A Street Fight," <u>Newsweek</u>, 29 April 2002, sec. International, p. 30 (2596 words) [database on-line]; available from Lexis-Nexis; accessed 29 August 2002.

[136] Congressional Research Service Report for Congress, <u>Intelligence and Law Enforcement: Countering Transnational Threats to the U.S.</u> (Washington, D.C.: The Library of Congress, January 16, 2001), p. CRS-4.

[137] Ibid.

[138] Bryan Bender, Kim Burger, and Andrew Koch, "Afghanistan: First Lessons," <u>Jane's Special Reports</u>, 14 December 2001; available from http://www.janes.com.html; Internet; accessed 12 September 2002.

[139] Ibid.

[140] Ibid.

[141] Dana Priest, "CIA Killed U.S. Citizen in Yemen Missile Strike," <u>The Washington Post</u>, 8 November 2002, Sec. A, p. 1.

[142] Vince Crawley and Amy Svitak, "Execution or Act of War: CIA Attack on Al-Qaida Leader Surprises Pentagon, Brings Up Ethical Concerns," <u>Army Times</u>, 18 November 2002, p. 10.

[143] Lieutenant Colonel Christopher F. Bentley, "Afghanistan: Joint and Coalition Fire Support in Operation Anaconda," <u>Field Artillery</u> (September-October 2002): 10.

[144] Ibid.

[145] These comments are based on the author's personal experience and discussions with Lieutenant Colonel Christopher F. Bentley in Uzbekistan and Afghanistan from December 2001 through June 2002. Lieutenant Colonel Bentley served as the Division Fire Support Coordinator (DFSCOORD), and the author served as the Staff Judge Advocate, for Coalition Joint Task Force – Mountain/10th Mountain Division (Light Infantry).

[146] *See generally* Joint Chiefs of Staff, <u>Interagency Coordination During Joint Operations</u>, Joint Publication 3-08 (Washington, D.C.: Joint Chiefs of Staff, 9 October 1996).

[147] Ibid.

[148] The ideas regarding Annex V are derived in part from Rick Westermeyer, "Theater Interagency Operations," briefing slides with scripted commentary, Carlisle Barracks, U.S. Army War College, December 2002. *See also generally* Joint Chiefs of Staff, <u>Interagency Coordination During Joint Operations</u>, Joint Publication 3-08 (Washington, D.C.: Joint Chiefs of Staff, 9 October 1996).

[149] Joint Chiefs of Staff, <u>Unified Action Armed Forces (UNAAF)</u>, Joint Publication 0-2 (Washington, D.C.: Joint Chiefs of Staff, 10 July 2001), xiii.

[150] *See* Joint Chiefs of Staff, <u>Interagency Coordination During Joint Operations</u>, Joint Publication 3-08 (Washington, D.C.: Joint Chiefs of Staff, 9 October 1996); *and* The White House, <u>Presidential Decision Directive/National Security Council 56, Managing Complex Contingency Operations</u> (May 1997); available from http://carlisle-www.army.mil/usacsl/divisions/pki/Political/Planning/interagency.htm; accessed 5 March 2003.

See also Association of the United States Army, Handbook for Interagency Management of Complex Contingency Operations (Washington, D.C., 13 August 1998); available from http://www.ausa.org/RAMPnew/PCR-PDD56Handbook.doc.htm; accessed 5 March 2003. This handbook is intended to institutionalize the mechanisms mandated by Presidential Decision Directive (PDD)-56. The procedures therein were derived from lessons learned from past U.S. participation in complex contingency operations and subsequent improvements made in the interagency planning process. The handbook provides a guide for those in the interagency that are or will be involved in planning such operations.

[151] Chuck McCutcheon, "Intelligence Authorization Calls for Greater Reliance on Spies and New Technology," Congressional Quarterly Weekly, 15 December 2001, p. 2993.

[152] Congressional Research Service Report for Congress, Intelligence and Law Enforcement: Countering Transnational Threats to the U.S. (Washington, D.C.: The Library of Congress, January 16, 2001), p. CRS-29.

[153] Suzanne C. Nielson, "Political Control Over the Use of Force: A Clausewitzian Perspective," The Letort Papers, U.S. Army War College (May 2001): 17, quoting Carl von Clausewitz, On War, trans. and eds. Michael Howard and Peter Paret (Princeton: Princeton University Press, 1976), 94. No serious research paper by a student at the U.S. Army War College can neglect to include a quote from Clausewitz.

BIBLIOGRAPHY

"Afghanistan - Countrywatch." Available from
    http://www.countrywatch.com/cw_topic.asp?vCOUNTRY=1&SECTION=SUB&TOPIC=PO
    PCO&T.html. Internet. Accessed 29 August 2002.

Ameringer, Charles D. U.S. Foreign Intelligence - The Secret Side of American History.
    Lexington, Massachusetts: Lexington Books, 1990.

Arkin, William M. "Warfare; Dressed -- and Equipped -- to Kill." Los Angeles Times, 4 August
    2002, M1. Database on-line. Available from ProQuest. Accessed 29 August 2002.

Associated Press. "CIA Plays High-Profile Military Role in Afghanistan with US-CIA-Shadow
    Army." Associated Press Worldstream, 20 May 2002, 1. Database on-line. Available from
    Lexis-Nexis. Accessed 29 August 2002.

Association of the United States Army. Handbook for Interagency Management of Complex
    Contingency Operations. Washington, D.C., 13 August 1998. Available from
    http://www.ausa.org/RAMPnew/PCR-PDD56Handbook.doc.htm. Accessed 5 March 2003.

Authorities of the Director of Central Intelligence. U.S. Code. Title 50, sec. 403-4 (2002).

Bender, Bryan, Kim Burger, and Andrew Koch. "Afghanistan: First Lessons." Jane's Special
    Reports, 14 December 2001. Available from http://www.janes.com.html. Internet.
    Accessed 12 September 2002.

Bentley, Lieutenant Colonel Christopher F. "Afghanistan: Joint and Coalition Fire Support in
    Operation Anaconda." Field Artillery (September-October 2002): 10.

"Bush's Address Announcing Military Strikes Against Afghanistan." World News Digest, 11
    October 2001. Available from http://www.2facts.com/stories/index/2001228130.asp.html.
    Internet. Accessed 29 August 2002.

Bush, George H.W. Statement on Signing the Intelligence Authorization Act, Fiscal Year 1991,
    14 August 1991. Available from http://bushlibrary.tamu.edu.papers/1991/91081401.html.
    Internet. Accessed 2 October 2002.

Central Intelligence Agency, Center for the Study of Intelligence. Central Intelligence: Origin and
    Evolution. Washington, D.C.: U.S. Government Printing Office, September 2001.

Chairman of the Joint Chiefs of Staff Seminar 2001. The Interagency Approach toward Complex
    Contingencies: Narrowing the Gaps Between Planning and Action. Carlisle Barracks,
    Pennsylvania: U.S. Army Peacekeeping Institute, 10-12 July 2001.

Charlton, Peter. "Conspiracy Theory." Courier Mail, 18 June 2002, 15. Database on-line.
    Available from Lexis-Nexis. Accessed 29 August 2002.

"CIA -- The World Factbook -- Afghanistan." Available from
    http://www.cia.gov.cia/publications/factbook/geos/af.html. Internet. Accessed 29 August
    2002.

Combatant Commands. U.S. Code. Title 10, sections 161-162, 164 (2002).

Combatant Commands: Assigned Forces; Chain of Command. U.S. Code. Title 10, sec. 162 (2002).

Commanders of Combatant Commands: Assignment; Powers and Duties. U.S. Code. Title 10, sec. 164(b)(1) and (d)(1) (2002).

Congress, United States. Senate Joint Resolution 23: Authorization for Use of United States Armed Forces, 107th Cong., 1st sess., 14 September 2002.

Congressional Record -- Senate. 107th Cong., 1st sess., 1 October 2001. Vol. 147, No. 129, sec. 9948.

Congressional Research Service Issue Brief for Congress. Intelligence Issues for Congress. Washington, D.C.: The Library of Congress, January 8, 2002.

Congressional Research Service Report for Congress. Intelligence and Law Enforcement: Countering Transnational Threats to the U.S. Washington, D.C.: The Library of Congress, January 16, 2001.

"Country Profile: Afghanistan." World News Digest, 29 August 2002. Available from http://www.2facts.com/ancillaries/index/c00002.asp.html. Internet. Accessed 29 August 2002.

Crawley, Vince and Amy Svitak. "Execution or Act of War: CIA Attack on Al-Qaida Leader Surprises Pentagon, Brings Up Ethical Concerns." Army Times, 18 November 2002, 10.

Department of Defense. Functions of the Department of Defense and its Major Components. Department of Defense Directive 5100.1. Washington, D.C.: U.S. Department of Defense, 1 August 2002.

Department of Defense. Law of War Program. Department of Defense Directive 5100.77. Washington, D.C.: U.S. Department of Defense, 9 December 1998.

Department of Defense. DOD Antiterrorism/Force Protection (AT?FP) Program. Department of Defense Directive 2000.12. Washington, D.C.: U.S. Department of Defense, 13 April 1999.

Drogin, Bob. "U.S. Had Plan for Covert Afghan Options Before 9/11." Los Angeles Times, 14. Database on-line. Available from Lexis-Nexis. Accessed 29 August 2002.

Dunlap, Brigadier General Charles J., Jr., USAF. "International Law and Terrorism: Some 'Qs and As' for Operators." The Army Lawyer. Department of the Army Pamphlet 27-50-357, October/November 2002.

Executive Order 12333--United States Intelligence Activities. 46 Federal Register 59941, 3 CFR, 1981 Comp., p. 200. Also available from http://www.cia.gov/cia/information/eo12333.html. Internet. Accessed 29 September 2002.

"Facts on Osama bin Laden." World News Digest, 29 August 2002. Available from http://www.2facts.com/ancillaries/index/b00222.asp.html. Internet. Accessed 29 August 2002.

Funding of Intelligence Activities. U.S. Code. Title 50, sec. 414 (2002).

Gates, Robert M. "CIA and Openness." Vital Speeches of the Day LVIII, no. 14 (1 May 1992): 430-431.

General Authorities of Agency. U.S. Code. Title 50, sec. 403f (2002).

Gertz, Bill. "Legal Concerns Make the CIA 'Risk Averse'." The Washington Times, 27 August 2002, 1.

Goodman, Alan E. "Reforming U.S. Intelligence." Foreign Policy no 67 (Summer 1987): 131, 133.

Green, John C. Secret Intelligence and Covert Action: Consensus in an Open Society. Strategy Research Project. Carlisle Barracks: U.S. Army War College, 19 March 1993.

Hersh, Seymour. "Manhunt: The Bush Administration's New Strategy in the War Against Terrorism." New Yorker, 23 December 2002.

"Hijacked Jets Destroy World Trade Center, Hit Pentagon: Text of President Bush's Statements." World News Digest, 13 September 2001. Available from http://www.2facts.com/stories/index/2001226370.asp.html. Internet. Accessed 29 August 2002.

Hodge, Nathan. "CIA's Predator Behavior is Cause for Concern." Newsday, 6 June 2002, A49. Database on-line. Available from Lexis-Nexis. Accessed 29 August 2002.

Holt, Pat M. Secret Intelligence and Public Policy - A Dilemma of Democracy. Washington, D.C.: Congressional Quarterly Inc., 1995.

Intelligence Authorization Act, Fiscal Year 1991. Statutes at Large 105, sec. 602 (1991) [Public Law 102-88, 14 August 1991].

Jay, John. "Federalist Number 64." Federalist Papers, 7 March 1788.

Joint Chiefs of Staff. Interagency Coordination During Joint Operations. Joint Publication 3-08. Washington, D.C.: Joint Chiefs of Staff, 9 October 1996.

Joint Chiefs of Staff. Unified Action Armed Forces (UNAAF). Joint Publication 0-2. Washington, D.C.: Joint Chiefs of Staff, 10 July 2001.

Kampeas, Ron. "CIA's Paramilitary Scores Successes." Associated Press Online, 20 May 2002, 1. Database on-line. Available from Lexis-Nexis. Accessed 29 August 2002.

Kessler, Ronald. Inside the CIA - Revealing the Secrets of the World's Most Powerful Spy Agency. New York: Pocket Books, 1992.

Kniazkov, Maxim. "CIA Creates Super Secret Hit Team to Target Terrorists Abroad." Agence France Presse, 4 June 2002, 1. Database on-line. Available from Lexis-Nexis. Accessed 29 August 2002.

Lumpkin, John J. "CIA Creates Terror Fighting Outfit." Associated Press Online, 3 June 2002, 1. Database on-line. Available from Lexis-Nexis. Accessed 29 August 2002.

McCutcheon, Chuck. "Intelligence Authorization Calls for Greater Reliance on Spies and New Technology." CQ Weekly, 15 December 2001, 2993.

Moore, J. Daniel. "CIA Support to Operation Enduring Freedom." Military Intelligence Professional Bulletin, vol. 28, iss. 3 (Jul-Sep 2002): 46. Database on-line. Available from ProQuest. Accessed 29 August 2002.

Nielson, Suzanne C. "Political Control Over the Use of Force: A Clausewitzian Perspective." The Letort Papers, U.S. Army War College (May 2001); quoting Carl von Clausewitz, On War, trans. and eds. Michael Howard and Peter Paret. Princeton: Princeton University Press, 1976.

Office of the Director of Central Intelligence U.S. Code. Title 50, sec. 403 (2002).

Oseth, John M. Regulating U.S. Intelligence Operations. Lexington: The University Press of Kentucky, 1985.

Pavitt, Jim, Deputy Director for Operations, Central Intelligence Agency. Text of Address to Duke University Law School Conference (as delivered), 11 April 2002. Available from http://www.cia.gov/cia/public_affairs/speeches/archives/2002/pavitt_04262002.html Internet. Accessed 17 March 2003.

Pavitt, Jim, Deputy Director for Operations, Central Intelligence Agency. Text of Remarks at the American Bar Association Standing Committee on Law and National Security Breakfast Program, 23 January 2003. Available from http://www.cia.gov/cia/public_affairs/speeches/ddo_speech_01232003.html Internet. Accessed 17 March 2003.

Pincus, Walter. "Missile Strike Carried Out With Yemeni Cooperation." The Washington Post, 6 November 2002, 10.

Presidential Approval and Reporting of Covert Actions. U.S. Code. Title 50, sec. 413b (2002).

Priest, Dana. "'Team 555' Shaped a New Way of War; Special Forces and Smart Bombs Turned Tide and Routed Taliban." The Washington Post - Final Edition, 3 April 2002, 1. Database on-line. Available from Lexis-Nexis. Accessed 29 August 2002.

Priest, Dana. "CIA Killed U.S. Citizen in Yemen Missile Strike." The Washington Post, 8 November 2002, 1.

Protection of Nature of Agency's Functions. U.S. Code. Title 50, sec. 403g (2002).

Ratnesar, Romesh. "Grading the Other War: Does our Fighting in Afghanistan Hold Any Lessons for a Battle with Iraq? A Report Card on the Afghan War's Uneven First Year."

<u>Time</u>, 14 October 2002. Database on-line. Available from
https://www.us.army.mil/portal/jhtml/earlyBird/Oct2002/e20021007grading.htm. Accessed
7 October 2002.

<u>Responsibilities of the Director of Central Intelligence</u>. U.S. Code. Title 50, sec. 403-3 (2002).

<u>Rewards for Information Concerning Terrorist Acts and Espionage; Definitions</u>. Title 18, <u>U.S.
Code</u>, Section 3077 (2002).

Rositzke, Harry. "America's Secret Operations: A Perspective." <u>Foreign Affairs</u> 53, no. 2
(January 1975): 344-345, 348.

Rositzke, Harry. <u>The CIA's Secret Operations</u>. New York: Reader's Digest Press, 1977.

Scarborough, Rowan. "Rumsfeld Gives 'Blank Sheet' to Update Special Operations." The
Washington Times, 21 November 2002, 15.

Scarborough, Rowan. "U.S. Forces Get OK to Use CIA Methods." <u>The Washington Times</u>, 1
October 2002, 1. Database on-line. Available from
https://www.us.army.mil/portal/jhtml/earlyBird/Oct2002/e20021001methods.htm.
Accessed 1 October 2002.

Schmidt, Susan and Thomas E. Ricks. "Pentagon Plans Shift in War on Terror: Special
Operations Command's Role to Grow with Covert Approach." <u>The Washington Post</u>, 18
September 2002, 1. Database on-line. Available from
https://www.us.army.mil/portal/jhtml/earlyBird/Sep2002/e20020918pentagon.htm.
Accessed 18 September 2002.

Shalikashvili, John M. <u>National Military Strategy of the United States of America</u>. Washington,
D.C.: The Pentagon, September 1997, 5.

Shanker, Thom and James Risen. "Rumsfeld Weighs New Covert Acts by Military Units." <u>The
New York Times, Late Edition - Final</u>, 12 August 2002, 1. Database on-line. Available from
Lexis-Nexis. Accessed 29 August 2002.

"Special Ops; Exploring New Uses is Appropriate." <u>Star Tribune (Minneapolis, MN)</u>, 19 August
2002, sec. A, p. 10 (432 words). Database on-line. Available from Lexis-Nexis. Accessed
29 August 2002.

Svitak, Amy. "Pentagon Blueprint to Guide Joint-Forces Tests, Development." <u>Army Times</u>, 11
November 2002, 24.

The CQ Researcher. <u>Intelligence Reforms</u>. Washington, D.C.: CQ Press, 25 January 2002, vol.
12, no. 3.

The White House. <u>National Security Strategy of the United States of America</u>. 10-12 (2002).
Available at http://www.whitehouse.gov/nsc/nssall.html.

The White House. <u>Presidential Decision Directive/National Security Council 56, Managing
Complex Contingency Operations</u> (May 1997). Available from http://carlisle-

www.army.mil/usacsl/divisions/pki/Political/Planning/interagency.htm. Accessed 5 March 2003.

Thomas, Evan and Colin Soloway. "A Street Fight." Newsweek, 29 April 2002, International 30. Database on-line. Available from Lexis-Nexis. Accessed 29 August 2002.

Turner, Stansfield. "Intelligence and Secrecy in an Open Society." The Center Magazine XIX, no. 2 (March/April 1986): 4.

Unified Combatant Command for Special Operations Forces. U.S. Code. Title 10, sec. 167, 167(d), 167(j) (2002).

United Press International. "CIA Plays Key Role." NewsMax Wires, 19 November 2001. Database on-line. Available from http://www.newsmax.com/archives/articles/2001/11/18/123101.shtml. Accessed 26 September 2002.

"U.S. Faces Islamic Radical Network." Strategic Forecasting LLC., 16 September 2001, p.1. Database on-line. Available from STRATFOR.com. Accessed 29 August 2002.

United States Special Operations Command. Special Operations in Peace and War. United States Special Operations Command Pub 1. Washington, D.C.: U.S. Special Operations Command, 25 January 1996, 2-2.

Waller, Douglas. "Inside the CIA's Covert Forces." Time, 10 December 2001, 56. Database on-line. Available from ProQuest. Accessed 29 August 2002.

Weisman, Jonathan. "CIA, Pentagon Feuding Complicates War Effort." USA Today, 17 June 2002, 11. Database on-line. Available from Lexis-Nexis. Accessed 29 August 2002.

Westermeyer. "Theater Interagency Operations." Briefing slides with scripted commentary. Carlisle Barracks: U.S. Army War College, December 2002.

Westfeldt, Amy. "9/11 Cost for NYC Tops $33 Billion." The Patriot-News, 13 November 2002, 8. The total worldwide economic loss impact has been estimated to top $600 billion, a "strategically significant" event according to remarks made by a speaker participating in the Commandant's Lecture Series at the Army War College in 2002.

"White House Target of Flight 93, Officials Say." CNN.COM, 23 May 2002. Available from http://www.cnn.com/2002/US/05/23/flight.93/index.html. Internet. Accessed 17 March 2003.

Williams, Frank J., Chief Justice. Supreme Court of Rhode Island. "Letter to the Editor: Abraham Lincoln and Al Qaeda." American Heritage, October 2002, 10-11.

Wittes, Benjamin. "Blurring the Line Between Cops and Spies." Legal Times, 9 September 1996.

Woodward, Bob. Bush at War. New York: Simon & Schuster, 2002.

Woodward, Bob. "CIA Told to Do 'Whatever Necessary' to Kill Bin Laden." <u>The Washington Post</u>, 21 October 2001. Available from <u>http://www.washingtonpost.com/ac2/wp-dyn/A27452-2001Oct20</u>. Internet. Accessed 26 September 2002.

Woodward, Bob. "Secret CIA Units Playing a Central Combat Role." <u>The Washington Post</u>, 18 November 2001, 1. Database on-line. Available from ProQuest. Accessed 29 August 2002.

"World Trade Center and Pentagon Terrorist Attacks: Transcript of Bush's Speech to Congress." <u>World News Digest</u>, 27 September 2002. Available from <u>http://www.2facts.com/stories/index/2001227310.asp.html</u>. Internet. Accessed 29 August 2002.

Xinhua General News Service. "Pentagon Weighs New Covert Acts by Special Military Units: Report." <u>Xinhua News Agency</u>, 12 August 2002. Database on-line. Available from Lexis-Nexis. Accessed 29 August 2002.